DATE DUE

# MANAGEMENT BY OBSTRUCTION

D1559086

# MANAGEMENT
# BY
# OBSTRUCTION

*or*

*How to Save Your Organization*
*From Needless Efficiency*

JARED *F.* HARRISON

PRENTICE-HALL, INC.
*Englewood Cliffs, N. J.*

Printed in the United States of America
Prentice-Hall International, Inc., London
Prentice-Hall of Australia, Pty. Ltd., Sydney
Prentice-Hall of Canada, Ltd., Toronto
Prentice-Hall of India Private Ltd., New Delhi
Prentice-Hall of Japan, Inc., Tokyo

10   9   8   7   6   5   4   3   2   1

---

Library of Congress Cataloging in Publication Data
Harrison, Jared F
    Management by obstruction.
    1.  Management.     2.   Efficiency, Industrial.
I.    Title.
HD31.H346        658.4        74–4470
ISBN  0–13–549055–3

# IN APPRECIATION

When I started to develop this text on Obstructive Management I felt that, because it is a new field of endeavor, valid examples would be difficult to uncover. Fortunately, this was not the case. In fact, literally everyone I spoke with, from my barber on up to University and Corporate Presidents, was overly anxious to tell me about an Obstructive Technique he had seen applied or was subjected to on the job. Their willingness to contribute anonymously shall not go unnoticed.

I particularly appreciated the cases provided by my friends and associates in the National Society of Sales Training Executives. It was heartwarming to hear them describe sophisticated Obstructive Techniques applied in their companies, and then vehemently request not to be quoted.

Finally, I want to express my greatest appreciation to Kay Varady, who knows many obstructionists, typed the final copy, suggested changes, and laughed a lot.

# FOREWARNED

Some of the brightest professors and trainers in the country are flooding the market with such informative texts as *Management by Results, Management by Objectives, Management by Commitment*—a plethora of books and articles all aimed at stamping out management inefficiency and designed to improve results and performance.

On campus, young scholars are striving for excellence and perfection. Those heading into management have been weaned on the thinking of such experts as Peter Drucker, George Odiorne, Saul Gellerman, and other advocates of management excellence.

Occasionally an author such as the noted Dr. Laurence J. Peter does flirt with negativism as in his revealing book, *The Peter Principle: Why Things Always Go Wrong* *, but even the learned Dr. Peter

* Wm. Morrow and Company, Inc., New York, 1968.

maintains that an individual should continually strive and seek to remain at his level of competence. Thus, he too becomes an advocate of excellence.

With all of this emphasis in literature, on the campus, and within industry on competence, there is a very real danger of over-competence. Have you ever stopped to think what might happen to our industrial system if, for even one day, every manager did a perfect job? The thought is appalling. The Gross National Product would go right out of sight. Thousands of consultants and managers whose livelihoods depend on inefficiency would be out of jobs. The marketplace could become quickly flooded with excellent quality goods and services far exceeding the demands. This, in turn, could cause the ultimate collapse of our entire system of free enterprise.

In the face of all this, it becomes dramatically clear that there is a crying need for a text that teaches the art of incompetence. Such a text would have a meaningful impact on present and future generations of managers, plus preserving forever the free enterprise system as we now know it.

Why is this text so important to present managers? Well, a close examination of any manager's job reveals that the average "good" manager spends approximately 80 percent of his time solving problems, while the other 20 percent is spent getting haircuts, playing golf, completing expense accounts, or generating memoranda and policies that create problems for subordinate managers. Thus, if there were no problems to solve, there would be little need for managers.

It therefore becomes critical to the survival of every manager to have an ongoing stream of problems flowing over him. Problem solution is the root to recognition, promotion, and prestige. So for the present-day manager, proper application of the techniques described in this text will prevent his problem stream from ever drying up. He will be able to generate all types of problems and then leap in and come up with positive solutions—thus gaining recognition, promotion, and prestige.

For the management student still in the university, this text provides successful strategies and techniques that have been used in decades past to screw up organizations. Thus, when he enters the management ranks, he will know how to insure the continuance of his managerial job.

Those in subordinate roles today will be able to identify and appreciate the finesse with which their managers apply Obstructive Techniques in a heroic effort to keep their organizations in a state of flux and preserve their managerial positions.

To help all students of Obstructive Management to quickly apply the various strategies, a unique format has been employed. After each strategy has been carefully defined, a specially prepared, often scripted case will be presented to illustrate an actual situation in which that technique can be used to accomplish obstructive results. These situations have all been used in the past by famously ineffective managers to successfully devastate profitable operations.

For convenient study, this text has been divided

into four sections, each representing a major function of the managerial job: planning, organizing, controlling, and evaluating. Listed under each of these sections are the obstructive strategies that the manager can use to create confusion, demoralize employees, and devastate the balance sheet.

All of the case material, approaches, and applications of these Obstructive Techniques are the results of years of research and observation. The techniques have been successfully employed in government, in industry, and in the hallowed halls of our educational institutions.

Exhaustive research, however, did not reveal the originators of these various strategies. Many have been handed down for generations, and the originators, regretfully, have been lost in oblivion. Thus, it has become necessary to give fictitious names to the practitioners and place them in various non-existent organizations. However, this should present no problem to the adept student who can readily relate the concepts to his own particular type of organization. Thus, with diligent practice and application of the strategies and techniques described in this text, runaway efficiency can be checked in time to preserve the critical balance of our economic system.

*Jared F. Harrison*

# CONTENTS

## CONTENTS

## Section III—CONTROLLING

## Section IV—EVALUATING

# I

## PLANNING

IN ANY MANAGEMENT
text, planning is generally recognized as the first
and foremost job of a successful manager. Without
proper planning, there is little hope of achieving any
meaningful results.

The same can be said for the importance of planning in Obstructive Management. To accomplish the proper degree of ineffectiveness, careful planning must be done. It is not something that can be treated casually since the techniques involved employ highly complex principles which must be studied repeatedly if they are to be used effectively. OBSTRUCTIVE PLANNING DOES NOT JUST HAPPEN!

Thus, the serious student is urged to learn the objectives and principles involved in each strategy, paying particular attention to the methods employed by the masterful practitioners who have successfully implemented each strategy in a real-world situation.

By taking this approach, it is possible to develop a repertoire of Obstructive Planning Techniques. Individual managerial style, personality, and organizational climate will, of course, dictate the most appropriate technique for any given situation.

# 1: STRATEGIC MYOPIA

THE PLANNING PRINCIPLE of Strategic Myopia is used most effectively by managers looking for a short-term gain in prestige or power while completely disregarding the long-range implications of a decision. Successful obstructive managers have used Strategic Myopia with excellent results in such areas as Product Planning, Personnel Development, and Sales Force Management; and it has often been found helpful when planning for research capabilities where the long-range objective is to have a zero return on investment.

The key element in applying this strategy is to look for an opportunity where immediate personal gain can result from the adoption of a short-range plan. Such a plan must seem good as long as the distant objectives are blurred and not highly visible. For Strategic Myopia to be effective, the manager must be able to convince both subordinates and superiors of the doctrine of linear extrapolation—or, "What's going on now is bound to continue."

To illustrate the proper employment of this technique, one needs only to review the case of the "Able-Bodied Equipment Corporation," where a classic example of Strategic Myopia was demonstrated by their General Sales Manager, Jason Fastclimber.

In 1971, the Able-Bodied Equipment Corporation decided to increase its production of flat flanges with the objective of getting more of them into the hands of ultimate consumers such as "do-it-yourself" homeowners. Actually, the suggestion had come from a Production Foreman who had dropped a note into the suggestion box saying: "We gotta get rid of some of these damn flanges. They're clogging up our warehouse and I can't use any more of them around my own home."

Jason Fastclimber, Chairman of the Suggestion Committee, had run across this suggestion at the bottom of the box after throwing away thirty earlier ones requesting his resignation.

Being a master at Obstruction Techniques, Jason immediately saw a chance to apply "Strategic Myopia." With the next Board of Directors meeting only a week away, he quickly involved his whole department plus three others in the preparation of a major presentation documenting the need for an additional sales organization to sell flat flanges directly to equipment supply houses.

His brilliant proposal recommended that a sales organization composed of thirty high-school graduates be immediately employed and that a Sales Trainer be hired to teach them how to inventory the dealers' stocks of flat flanges and to take orders from dealers requesting restocking. Each salesman was to be trained to walk into a dealer's organization and ask the question, "You don't need any more flat flanges today, do you?" And if the dealer said "Yes," the salesman was to find out how many he needed, write it out, and take it back to the home office where it could be duplicated into twenty-five copies prior to shipment of the flat flanges.

Jason's proposal laid great emphasis on how his plan would relieve the clogged warehouse immediately by pushing the inventory on out to the dealers. He then recommended an incentive compensation plan for the salesmen based on how many times a day they asked the all-important question, "You don't need any more flat flanges today, do you?" Jason's next suggestion was that he be promoted to Vice-President of Marketing, which would be befitting to his new set of responsibilities as the leader of this sales organization.

Because of the clogged warehouse situation, the Board immediately approved Jason's plan and promoted him to Vice-President of Marketing. Soon the flat flanges moved out of the warehouse and into the dealers' inventories; each month a salesman would stop by to ask the dealers if any more flat flanges were needed and then inventory the stock on hand.

7

Jason was extremely happy, and in fact was able to expand his sales organization to forty salesmen by 1972. At this point, Jack Dollar, the Comptroller, mentioned casually to Jason one day in the men's room that the out-of-pocket cost to support the sales organization was slowly bankrupting the company and that he planned to bring it up at the next Board meeting.

This was exactly what Jason had been waiting to hear. His original Strategic Myopia tactic had planned for just such an eventuality. For the next two weeks, he involved his staff, plus two other departments, in the preparation of a major presentation that recommended the dissolving of the sales organization. In its place, a recorded telephone message would be called in to each dealer once a month inquiring, "You don't need any more flat flanges this month, do you?" If the dealer did, indeed, need some, he could record his order on magnetic tape without involving a salesman. A prepared chart showed how the company could realize an immediate improvement in their bottom-line profits by this reduction in the overhead costs of the sales organization. The recommendations were quickly approved, and as a result of the huge savings Jason was promoted to Executive Vice-President of Marketing.

Now for the student of Obstructive Managerial Techniques, this case is an excellent example. By stressing the short-term or strategic gains to be made, Jason effectively fogged the minds of the Board of Directors and got himself promoted each time. Each new decision he made managed to cost the company a considerable amount of money, yet not totally bankrupt it.

Just recently it was learned that Jason now has the Marketing Division, plus three other sections, involved in the preparation of another presentation which will suggest that a computer terminal be placed in each dealer's organization, connected to a new central office computer at Able-Bodied Equipment Corporation. Thus, the computers can ask each other if they need any flat flanges this month. This newest suggestion should get Jason the Presidency.

So, in review, when applying the planning technique of Strategic Myopia, look for a situation where an immediate personal gain can be made by totally disregarding the long-range effects of a decision. Make sure that you are able to correctly estimate a future decision which will even further increase your prestige and power. The most likely areas for such opportunities are in sales management, as illustrated by Able-Bodied Equipment Corporation—or in product management where, with a little Strategic Myopia, you can manage to develop the wrong product at the wrong time and sell at the wrong price.

# 2: LONG-RANGE DISCONTINUITY

THE TECHNIQUE OF Long-Range Discontinuity has been most effectively employed by short-term company Presidents or managers who seem to join a new organization, stay approximately two years, and then get promoted to more responsible positions in another company. It has often been suggested that this group of highly talented obstructionists belong to some form of un-structured association so that they can change jobs with each other every two years, always at a higher salary. Research, however, has failed to prove the existence of such an association. Nevertheless, it is a remarkable coincidence that all such practitioners of Long-Range Discontinuity seem to know each other and are familiar with the work done in a variety of corporations.

To the potential practitioner of Long-Range Discontinuity, a superficial knowledge of a wide variety of managerial strategies and techniques is required. Another important, though less essential attribute is the correct physical appearance. The most successful disciples of this strategy all seem to be six feet tall, lean, lanky, square-jawed, and slightly graying at the temples. Horn-rimmed glasses are sometimes added to complete the proper image. Quite often, an initial will be used in place of a first name and such appendages as "the Third" are added to complete the picture.

One of the all-time great practitioners of Long-Range Discontinuity, P. Brian Bleary III, has just retired from active practice after a career which had led him through fifteen companies in the past thirty years. Because of his success and the insight and guidance he could bring to future practitioners of Long-Range Discontinuity, P. Brian Bleary III was interviewed in his palatial home deep in the Brazilian jungle. . . .

AUTHOR: Thank you, Mr. Bleary, for granting me this interview in in your hideaway in Brazil.

P. B. BLEARY: Not at all. I am glad to help in the production of this valuable text.

AUTHOR: Tell me, does your name play an important role in your work?

P. B. BLEARY: Yes, it certainly does. Can you guess how?

AUTHOR: Well, by using just the initial "P" at the start of it, I would guess that it would prevent subordinates from calling you, "Hey, P."

P. B. BLEARY: You guessed it! This immediately puts subordinates in an uneasy position, not knowing just what to call me.

AUTHOR: I can see how that might help. Also, "the Third" has a certain ring to it.

P. B. BLEARY: Yes. Actually, I am the only P. B. Bleary, but no one ever bothered to question it.

AUTHOR: How did you start out to become the world's greatest practitioner of Long-Range Discontinuity?

P. B. BLEARY: Well, I met a group of men who were over six feet tall, lean, lanky, square-jawed, who sometimes wear horn-rimmed glasses and are graying at the temples at an association meeting, and I liked their style of operation. They told me they were professional managers and asked if I would like to join their group.

AUTHOR: You mean, then, there *is* an

13

|                |                                                                                 |
|----------------|---------------------------------------------------------------------------------|
|                | association of professional managers?                                           |
| P. B. BLEARY:  | It's a very loose association, and we all are known only by our first initials. |
| AUTHOR:        | Can you explain for the managers who will be working with this text just how the technique of Long-Range Discontinuity is applied? |
| P. B. BLEARY:  | First of all, you have to select a reasonably capable management team of young, square-jawed, lean, lanky, six-footers with horn-rimmed glasses and gray at the temples whom you can take with you to any new position you may get. It is helpful if one of the team members has some knowledge of production and if another is reasonably familiar with some sales strategies. |
| AUTHOR:        | After you have formed your team, what kind of a company do you look for?        |
| P. B. BLEARY:  | Usually, I get the name of one from the association. But if no such opening is available, I try to find a company that is |

14

having difficult times and whose stockholders are clamoring for reorganization.

AUTHOR: What is your next step?

P. B. BLEARY: Here's where the strategy is very quickly applied. Take your team and convince the old-time Chairman of the Board that what he needs is a complete reorganization and shaking-up of the company. It is best to bargain for a two-year contract that will give you fifty percent of the profits plus your salary at the end of the two-year period.

AUTHOR: Is the two-year time period significant?

P. B. BLEARY: Yes, highly important, since it is impossible to sustain the technique of Long-Range Discontinuity much past the two-year mark.

AUTHOR: I see. This at least guarantees you'll be on some payroll for a two-year period.

P. B. BLEARY: Exactly. And that's what is needed. Once hired, take your team and install them in key positions. Then, the next step is crucial to the ultimate success of Long-Range Discontinuity.

AUTHOR: Please explain it carefully for our readers.

P. B. BLEARY: The first day on the job, you must search through all the personnel records of individuals in the home office, and judiciously select only the mediocre performers who show little or no future potential.

AUTHOR: Why look for these individuals?

P. B. BLEARY: It's obvious. They won't be expecting a promotion, and if you grant them even a small raise and a large title, they can be completely dominated and will not cause any problems for the next two years.

AUTHOR: What kinds of jobs do you give these individuals?

P. B. BLEARY: I make them Directors reporting to my team in such areas as finance, personnel, planning, and production.

AUTHOR: Doesn't this have an adverse effect on the good, intelligent managers left in the company?

P. B. BLEARY: Exactly. They all usually resign, thus leaving me a clear field.

AUTHOR: What's the next step?

P. B. BLEARY: It's simple. Knowing that I've got two years and a contract for fifty percent of the profit plus my salary, all I've got to do is make the bottom-line profits look good.

AUTHOR: How is this accomplished?

P. B. BLEARY: First of all, I cut out all advertising. Next, I cut back production on all items except the most profitable. The third step is to reduce sales expense by cutting out forty percent of the sales organization. Meanwhile, my team is cutting back on such nonessentials as long-range product development, market-research information, training and development, etc.

AUTHOR: Doesn't this cause some concern on the part of the Board of Directors?

P. B. BLEARY: Yes, sometimes, but they are easily placated because my team is taught to talk in terms of long-range results. If the pressure gets too much, we in-

17

stall various approaches such as new computer applications to maintain inventory control, new report-writing procedures, etc. This normally does the job of keeping everybody happy, causing them to think we are doing careful planning for future growth.

AUTHOR: What about employee morale?

P. B. BLEARY: This can be handled quite easily by sending out numerous bulletins and making speeches stressing a "new team" and "new ball game" concept. All employees are invited to get behind this new group who is going to help their company make a leap into the future. Such phrases as "quantum jump" and "giant step forward" seem to go over quite well. Another technique is to announce the start of a long-range study on incentive compensation for all employees. This seems to cause a tremendous morale lift among the workers.

AUTHOR: Do you actually start such a study?

P. B. BLEARY: Of course. However, it is such a long-range study that its completion date usually arrives about a year after I have moved on to my next assignment.

AUTHOR: How do you know when it's time to leave?

P. B. BLEARY: Well, at the end of the two-year period, the financial man on my team prepares a large presentation showing the tremendous jump which has taken place in bottom-line profits, and this is submitted to the Board. Normally, the Board will grant me and my team some added incentive to stay on for another two-year term, which we delicately turn down. Meanwhile, through our association, we have identified a slightly larger corporation that is about to have a stockholders' meeting and request the removal of their existing President. With accolades from the present company, it's relatively easy to take my entire team on to its next assignment.

AUTHOR: What happens to the company you've just left?

19

P. B. BLEARY: Well, obviously, the mediocre management that we trained to fill our slots takes over, and in no time at all, they are ready for another association manager and his team to come in and "straighten out their company."

AUTHOR: One final question, P. B. Why are you living in Brazil?

P. B. BLEARY: I like it down here. And, of course, I can't be extradited.

It is hoped that from this interview with the leading practitioner of the technique of Long-Range Discontinuity you will be able to apply this system on *your* job. The key elements to remember in its application are the securing of a two-year contract to accomplish an objective, a well-balanced and fairly knowledgeable support team to take with you, plus the managerial ability to know which nonessentials to cut out so that no disasters will befall the company prior to the end of your two-year contract. Obviously, it helps if you are over six feet tall, lean, lanky, square-jawed, have a pair of horn-rimmed glasses, and are graying at the temples. The association is difficult to join, but after several successful two-year assignments, they will seek you out as a member.

# 3: INNOVATIVE COMPLACENCY

PRACTITIONERS OF OB-structive Management have long defined Innovative Complacency as a planning strategy which creates the illusion of innovation while clinging steadfastly to the principles of the status quo. These same practitioners recommend consideration of this strategy whenever pressures for "change" seem to be building up during a planning or forecasting meeting.

One of the prerequisites for applying this concept properly is the ability to recognize quickly the existence of such pressures for change. Usually they can be identified by an on-the-spot, subjective evaluation of both the proposal and its source. For example, if a young, aggressive Sales Manager, who has a recent M.B.A. degree, suggests that, "Company philosophy should be realigned from product orientation toward an empathetic approach to customers' satisfactions," you can be pretty sure that he's a trouble-maker intent on disrupting the status quo.

Obviously, your first impulse is to fire him on the spot. But this would make him eligible for unemployment benefits and could cause further dissension among other young, aggressive M.B.A.'s. Thus, it is far wiser to employ immediately the "Strategem of Innovative Complacency," which will result in the young M.B.A.'s eventual promotion to a position of total impotence.

To understand fully how Innovative Complacency is accomplished, one only has to review the case of Casper Clothnot, President of Celluloid Collars Limited.

For forty years, Casper and CCL had had a happy co-existence. Casper had been promoted to the Presidency suddenly one day when his father, Clarence, met him in the corridor and took a liking to him.

Casper continued in the fine family tradition of complacency by awarding his brother the advertising contract and making himself Chief Engineer, in addition to being President, and promoting a loyal clerk (his cousin) to be Treasurer.

Sales had never been a problem, since most of the buyers preferred to deal directly with the President. Even though the market had diminished in recent years, Casper continued to make a modest profit by offering a high-quality product at a low unit cost. This was accomplished by making only one model which could be mass produced.

Casper Clothnot's problems started one day on

the golf course when he won a match from his Uncle Fred for the senior championship. Fred, whose son had just received his M.B.A. from Harvard, agreed not to tell the Tournament Committee that Casper used his foot to get out of a sand trap if Casper would hire his son as Sales Manager.

From his first day on the job, Fred's son, Binky LaMonte, proposed some organizational changes. Having been weaned on the tenets of the marketing concept, he quickly reviewed the organizational chart and found to his horror that CCL was "product," not "customer" oriented!

At the very next staff meeting, Binky arrived armed with charts and graphs illustrating a totally new, innovative organization, new markets, and a new customer-oriented product line.

His brilliant presentation proved that CCL was not in the celluloid-collar business but in the "neck-covering industry"! And as anyone knows, this is not even limited to human necks. Any neck is a potential customer, be it that of a giraffe, bottle, or spit of land.

To serve this huge market, Binky proposed that he be made Vice-President of Marketing and that a Marketing Services Department be created to combine advertising, promotion, market research, and marketing planning—all of which would, of course, report to him. Next he proposed that he hire three Sales Managers to be in charge of neck sales in each potential market area, animal, vegetable, and mineral.

As Casper Clothnot listened to the presentation, he

realized that it was time to apply Innovative Complacency!

Some of his friends at the Broken Rock Country Club were Presidents of companies that had Marketing Departments and Casper rather liked the new name Marketing, instead of the old-fashioned Sales. But his problem was how to "go-a-Marketing" without disrupting the status quo—or to put it another way, how to look progressive while doing the same old, comfortable job and at the same time get rid of Binky.

Here's how this master of Innovative Complacency accomplished his objectives:

1. He had his brother call a press conference of trade media.
2. He announced with banner headlines that "CCL Goes Marketing."
3. He released a picture of a smiling Binky standing in front of a door labeled Vice-President of Marketing with the caption, "Binky LaMonte leads CCL into the neck-covering industry. Can mean a quantum jump for CCL."
4. He started reviewing files of lower relatives who, if promoted, would not disrupt the status quo.

The end result was exactly as planned. Binky was quickly hired away by a conglomerate who needed a neck-covering, marketing-oriented M.B.A. Casper then promoted a third cousin from engineering to the position of Vice-President of Marketing, and thus was able to brag to his friends at the Country Club that he, too, had a Marketing Department. And Casper was able to continue his single product line, but now he had the collars painted different colors and some with stripes so that he could become "customer-oriented."

So, if you are faced with a situation which is apt to disrupt the status quo, try applying the planning concept of Innovative Complacency. Normally, it is done by congratulating the innovator, grabbing headlines for the idea, quickly screening for a reliable replacement, preferably a distant relative, and then maintaining business as usual.

# 4: COGNITIVE DISCORDANCY

IN THIS CHAPTER, WE will be reviewing one of the more important planning strategies guaranteed to foul up any organization; one which is closely related to the basic objective of this book. The technique we will be exploring is that of Cognitive Discordancy, which recognizes the basic need to avoid efficiency and promote discord over a long period of time, thus insuring numerous managerial jobs for the future. It is highly important that a manager intentionally defer any possibility of solving an existing problem through the application of Cognitive Discordancy, so that he can either retire or be promoted. This obviously takes some long-range planning when faced with the need for a decision that could lead to greater efficiency in the long run.

A common definition attributed to Cognitive Discordancy is "to create discord with intent." In practice, some scholars have termed it simply, "knowing you are going to screw it up." The difficulty with the short definition, however, is that one tends to confuse this planning principle with the controlling principle of Conscientious Incompetence, the latter being a day-to-day method of managing.

With this somewhat practical working definition now before us, let's examine a case taken from industry which firmly demonstrates the actual use of this planning principle.

Pintronics Incorporated is a multidivisional conglomerate whose main product thrust until recent years had been in the production and distribution of high-grade pins. Actually, up until the late 1960's it had been merely called Pinston's Pins, from the family name which had stood it in good stead since the early 1700's.

In 1969, the then Chief Executive Officer and Chairman of the Board, Colonel Percival Pinston, was pinned beneath his own car and was quickly succeeded on the Board of Directors by his son, Finster Pinston.

Finster, having recently graduated from an Advanced Management course, changed the company name to Pintronics so as to be more in tune with space-age technology. He also set in motion a wide-ranging product diversification program based on the new company's slogan, which Finster originated: "If it has a pin, it's a business we're in."

The diversification program carried Pintronics

from its traditional high-quality straight-pin, diaper-pin, and hairpin business into such exotic fields as the manufacture of golf pins, kingpins, belaying pins, pinball machines, pinion wheels, and surgical pins. It was even rumored that Finster was negotiating for a stable of Pinto ponies. Another move of Finster's was to redesignate the home office as the Pinnacle.

Despite this rapid diversification (and grumblings among some of the workers claiming that the Pinnacle was inhabited by pinheads and their paychecks resembled pin money), success did come to Pintronics.

Part of this success, Finster felt, was due to his insistence that with each new acquisition and each new product line, a reliable service department, headed up by representatives of corporate engineering, be established to service the specific product. With engineers in control, the service departments could often modify products to "fit customer needs" and regularly blame the Sales department for selling the wrong products or the manufacturing department for poor quality control. Also, the engineers could spend hours with their customers' engineers, comparing such important things as slide rules or mutually redesigning each other's products.

All in all, the operation pleased Finster and provided him with numerous opportunities to exercise his managerial talents of problem solving. Disputes continually developed between Sales and Engineering which Finster himself felt he should resolve;

numerous confrontations between engineers and manufacturing personnel over quality issues also required managerial arbitration.

Finster also was pleased by just the right amount of calls from irate customers claiming that their companies' engineers were spending so much time discussing redesigns with Pintronics' engineers that work was backing up. Finster was now provided with many excellent opportunities to intervene.

He particularly enjoyed these customer complaints, since they usually required extensive trips to "smooth out customer relations" in some exotic place such as Pebble Beach, the Doral Country Club, or Las Vegas—where he would take the customers to inspect the pin placements of each hole.

All in all, the present organizational system was working quite well. It had created many managerial jobs and many problems to be solved, and showed definite signs of becoming even more complex in the long range. Finster's nicely screwed-up world, however, was soon to be threatened. In a weaker moment, several months back, he had approved applications by both his Vice-President of Manufacturing and his Vice-President of Marketing to attend separate seminars on the subject of planning given by a nationally recognized organization. At the time, Finster thought little of it, since he really didn't expect any great changes in their behavior as a result of attending such seminars.

Finster knew both of his Vice-Presidents extremely well, having handpicked them from the most ineffective management candidates he could find, and felt he would be able to predict their approaches to organizational development. After all, planning means only the development of plans, which in turn could be reviewed and rejected if they indeed seemed threatening. What Finster could not predict, however, was that both executives, once allowed a glimpse of the outside world and how other companies were organized, would develop dreams of grandeur—returning to take a new look at the organizational structure beneath them, each with a view toward how he might be promoted to the nonexistent position of Executive Vice-President.

Shortly after the two Vice-Presidents returned from their seminars, both suggested to Finster that they immediately start work on redevelopment plans for their own organizations. Seeing no immediate threat, Finster agreed and even went so far as to set a deadline for the first planning review. He did at least have the presence of mind to schedule separate meetings with each Vice-President: This way he could avoid any chance of their working together and also keep from each what the other one was planning to do—which in the long range would cause further opportunities for management expertise on Finster's part.

The first planning review was scheduled with the Vice-President of Marketing. Finster faced this review with an air of quiet assurance, since he felt that the major items to be planned were well within his capabilities to control. The first item presented, which Finster quickly approved, was a recommendation to increase the quotas assigned to the sales representatives. The next proposal involved a new and much expanded advertising and sales promotion campaign, consisting of pinup calendars to be mailed to all existing accounts and potential accounts in some new marketing areas. Finster approved the idea of the pinup calendars but cut the requested dollars, saying that he personally would help in the interviewing of prospective calendar art.

The third recommendation involved increasing the sales training for the existing sales force. This Finster saw as a potential threat since it might inspire the salesmen to attempt to move on up through the ranks to managerial positions, so a very limited budget was approved for this purpose.

Then a major problem developed. The Marketing Vice-President presented an idea that caused Finster to stop playing with his pinwheel and sit up and listen. The key element of the plan called for a reorganizational effort that would place the service operation directly under the Vice-President of Marketing. This plan would hopefully provide a team effort between sales and service through the development of sales service specialists by product lines. The Marketing Vice-President was quick to point out that this simple move could increase market responsiveness and at the same time create career development paths from Service to Sales, therefore boosting the morale of the Service Engineers.

Finster realized immediately that this plan could

eliminate many of the interesting managerial opportunities which he presently enjoyed. It also would increase the stature of the Vice-President of Marketing and firmly establish him as the logical candidate for the nonexistent position of Executive Vice-President.

Faced with this potential threat, Finster decided to table his decision and to "take it under careful consideration," meaning in fact that he hoped the problem would just go away.

After the Marketing Vice-President had left the office, Finster reviewed this startling plan in his own mind. The concept of product-line sales service specialists could lead to a far more efficient organization, but Finster's opportunities to handle irate customers would be limited.

It was then that the words of his late father, Colonel Percival Pinston, who had pioneered ineffective management, came back to him: "When faced with a situation that clearly indicates a threat, resort to the strategy of Cognitive Discordancy and look for ways where discord can be created with the full knowledge that it will eventually screw up the organization." Finster realized that Cognitive Discordancy was clearly the proper method of handling the threat he was now facing. He had to seemingly allow the Marketing Vice-President an attempt at reorganizing the Service Department while at the same time insuring that the results of this reorganization would be ineffective or create discord between Marketing and some other major operation. The answer came to Finster just before the next scheduled planning review with the Manufacturing Vice-President.

The Manufacturing Vice-President's plans were routine, calling for such mundane approaches as increasing capacity in certain operations, furthering quality control and safety regulations, and developing a new nine-hole golf course close to the Pinnacle to test pin placement during lunch hour. Finster saw that none of these presented a great threat to him or to the overall efficiency of the organization. Quickly approving these plans, he then started his approach to the application of Cognitive Discordancy.

With the Manufacturing Vice-President seemingly relaxed (thinking he had won the favor of the boss), Finster casually brought up the concept of a potential reorganization of the service function. Finster wondered out loud what might happen if an organization such as Manufacturing controlled all of the service operations for Pintronics. Finster discussed the possibility that this just might insure conformity across all product lines and could lead to a consolidated parts warehouse which might eliminate some duplication. Cross-training of servicemen would create generalists who would be able to service all the Pintronics products. All of this might be a reality with Service reporting through Manufacturing.

At this point, the Manufacturing Vice-President caught the spirit of Finster's message and suggested that career paths within the service field be developed from production on through to outside servicing, stating that this concept of centralization might benefit the Pintronics customers, giving them just one place to call for service. He also recalled that recently he had met several other Manufacturing Vice-Presidents at the seminar who were responsible for the total service effort within their companies and who were being considered for promotion to Executive Vice-President.

All of this seemed to stimulate the Manufacturing Vice-President tremendously, and Finster smiled happily knowing he had sewn the seeds for Cognitive Discordancy.

Finster asked the Manufacturing Vice-President to go back to his office and draw up a full-scale plan proposing the transfer of service to the manufacturing operation and an outline of the benefits that would accrue from such a move, such as a consolidated parts warehouse, the cross-training function, and the career paths for service people from production on through to outside servicing.

When the now-elated Manufacturing Vice-President left, Finster began to plan his next move: A meeting was set up between the Vice-President of Manufacturing, the Vice-President of Marketing, and Finster to discuss the future plans of the service operation.

Here it is important for the student of Obstructive Management to fully recognize the objectives of such a meeting. To implement Cognitive Discordancy, Finster had to create the impression of deep concern for both plans, show full awareness of the potential benefits, and yet reach a decision for implementation that would create discord for which Finster himself could not be blamed.

Finster's execution of this meeting was a model of how the truly professional obstructive manager makes the strategy Cognitive Discordancy work. He sent out a memo from his office to the Vice-President of Marketing and Vice-President of Manufacturing requesting that both meet with him to discuss potential reorganization of the service operation. Neither manager knew that the other had presented a plan for the potential reorganization. Thus, each came to the meeting thinking it was his own plan which was going to be discussed. When Finster revealed that two plans were under consideration for reorganization, this immediately set up a stress situation.

Finster then asked each Vice-President to disclose his recommendation for the ultimate reassignment of the service operation. While they were going through their descriptions, Finster listened attentively and took copious notes. At the completion of the proposals, Finster quickly took control of the meeting and announced his decision.

The decision was to create a pilot operation in each sales region while maintaining the present engineering service force to evaluate operating results. In one region, manufacturing would be responsible for consolidation of all service operations and in another region, marketing would be responsible for the product-line service operation, reporting to the Regional Marketing Manager. With Engineering acting as the evaluator of this pilot operation, it would not take long to see who captured the largest portion of the pin service market in each region.

Finster's plan was reluctantly accepted by both Vice-Presidents. Each left the meeting feeling that it was up to him to prove the benefit of his plan, which could lead to his possible promotion. As far as Finster was concerned, he had accomplished all of his objectives. First, by calling it a "pilot program," the idea could be given a try without any real expectations of it working, and both projects could be dropped at any time. Second, three different approaches to service would create more management jobs, thus produce more problems for higher management to solve. Third, competition between groups would cause even more customer complaints, thus creating further opportunity to "smooth out customer relations" in even more exotic golfing locations. Fourth, no one could pin the blame on Finster Pinston, for he had given every plan a chance. Fifth, Finster could keep pilot-testing these plans until he safely retired.

The student of Obstructive Management Techniques should note that while this case illustrates a true master of Cognitive Discordancy at work, this same strategy does not necessarily have to be applied at such a high level within an organization. It works equally well at department or section level, provided that the manager creates a climate in which planning is an important function of the everyday effort.

Whenever planning is applied and the content of

the proposed plans seems threatening, consider using Cognitive Discordancy. Keep in mind that your objective is to create discord, but at the same time, do it with intent. At the lower levels of the echelon, this can be adroitly applied if goals or objectives are being established by your subordinates. Whenever these goals or objectives seem in any way to threaten your position over the long run or tend to elevate the importance of the subordinate out of proportion to his real worth from your point of view, then be sure to take action similar to the approach used in the Finster Pinston case.

One of the major elements to keep in mind is the use of "pilot" programs or trial approaches. Rarely, if ever, is a pilot program expected to succeed, at least in its initial design. The very word "pilot" implies that it is something you are going to try without really expecting dramatic results. Thus, through the creation of pilot programs—particularly if they parallel or overlap each other—a department manager can creat discord within his operation, which in the eyes of his higher management gives him the opportunity to straighten it all out and take control.

The student of Obstructive Management will find conscious application of Cognitive Discordancy an excellent way to create disorder within an organization and at the same time serve the management status quo, so essential to the continuance of ineffective management.

# 5: CALCULATED REACTIONISM

Management student who is looking for ways to move on up the executive ranks, the strategy of Calculated Reaction is probably one of the most widely applied. It is by far the easiest of all Obstructive Techniques to install in any organization, particularly at some of the lower-level positions—because it is accomplished by simply doing nothing. In fact, it is not uncommon for managers to be given credit for the application of Calculated Reactionism when, in reality, the evident lack of planning in their departments was just an oversight.

Thus, the student must be careful to examine all the elements surrounding an unplanned decision to identify a true Calculated Reactionism application. The technique for establishing this planning strategy is the conscious avoidance of *all* planning, coupled with the ability to react rapidly and creatively once something goes wrong.

Actually, this ability for quick reaction (or even overreaction) is the key element. The reactionist manager personally takes care of any emergencies that come up in his department. He is an expert at putting out fires and always winds up looking like a hero in spite of the huge extra costs often incurred during the implementation of his remedies.

In recent years, practitioners of Obstructive Management Techniques have tended more and more to recognize Calculated Reactionism as a temporary strategy to be applied fairly early in a career and then abandoned for some of the other more sophisticated Obstructive Techniques. The prime reason for this view is that proper application of Calculated Reactionism requires a great deal of physical and mental energy, which in turn takes its toll on the individuals using this technique. There have been some successful cases reported where managers have used the strategy throughout their lifetime. But generally speaking, if you are able to solve one or two major problems resulting directly from a lack of planning, this should be sufficient to get you promoted and allow you to switch to a less physically and mentally demanding style of Obstructive Planning.

To give the student a better understanding of the characteristics of a good Calculated Reactionist and facilitate easier identification of a manager who may be practicing this strategy, the following physical, mental, office, and personal characteristics were noted by a research team that visited a manager who has spent the major portion of his working life applying this technique. Their findings are as follows:

## PHYSICAL

Overweight from many drinks and rich meals celebrating snap judgments

High blood pressure, high pulse rate from constant pressure

Slightly balding from tearing out hair

Heavy smoker

Headache-prone, caused usually by subordinates

Red sunken eyes from lack of sleep worrying about problems

## MENTAL

Always in a hurry to get nowhere in particular

Pessimistic, feels that whatever will go wrong will

Looks for *problems,* not opportunities

Irritable

Dislikes slow-moving and slow-talking people

Feels he is a doer, action-oriented

Loves to reflect on past glories

Resents structure, mistrusts others

## OFFICE AND PERSONAL APPEARANCE

Unkempt, disheveled

Cluttered desk, wrong date on calendar

Unfiled correspondence stacked all over office

Tie does not match suit

Shirt sleeves rolled up

Cigarette dangles from his mouth

Ashes all over the desk

Phone with four lines and a speaker attachment

Atmosphere much like a command post under attack, or the bridge of a sinking ship

Staff members rush in and out asking, "What are we going to do about this?"

Barks commands, detailed orders

Subordinates never allowed to take any action; when questioned, they always say, "I'll check it out with the boss."

From this profile, the student can see that the Calculated Reactionist planner is, indeed, a one-man show, and because of this he is under constant strain.

While the profile given above might be sufficient for a student to identify a planner who operates under this strategy, regrettably it doesn't give a very broad view of how he actually performs on any given business day. For this reason, the author felt it necessary to spend some time with one of the more famous non-planners and record a time study covering his actions and reactions.

Thus, the following time log covers one hour in the life of Stu Sufferlong, General Contractor and partner in the famous firm of Sufferlong and Sweat. The project under construction was the Bilkertown Bank building; the date, March 17; the time, 0700 hours; the weather, cold, overcast with intermittent rain.

0700    Stu arrives at trailer office, parks Cadillac behind cement mixer.

0705    Plugs in coffeepot, short circuits electrical lines, which blacks out trailer.

0710    Starts auxiliary generator to light trailer and heat coffee.

0715    Foreman rushes in yelling about water seeping into the basement. Says, "What are we going to do about it and where the hell are the pumps you were going to order?"

0717    Stu inspects basement, falls into water, confirms that there is indeed water seeping in.

0720     Stu rushes back to trailer, calls pumps salesman at home—asks for pump demonstration; hints he *might* buy if satisfied.

0730     Phone rings: Plumbing contractor has run out of pipe for men's room. Stu suggests using electrical conduit embedded in the concrete floor—no one will ever see it anyway.

0740     Safe installer rushes in, complains that reinforced floor has been installed in lobby rather than in vault —vault floor won't support the safe. Stu changes plans, making the vault the President's office—calls decorator to drape the outside of the safe to make it a "center of attraction."

0750     Cement-truck driver reports that he has backed up over Stu's Cadillac and accidentally filled it with concrete—Stu orders concrete car to be used as fill against rear wall to stop water seepage—adds cost of new Cadillac to job, calling it "prefabricated drainage system."

0800     Stu's wife calls telling him she is leaving him and going back to mother— Stu calls redhead at Cadillac agency, sets up a date, and orders a new Cadillac.

0805    Author leaves for rest in country.

For the student viewing an obstructive manager and applying this technique for the first time, it might seem that this one hour's description of catastrophic events could all have been avoided by simple planning. This is obviously true. However, if Stu had planned appropriately and everything had gone extremely smoothly, the results of his planning might not have equaled the results he obtained. Thus, it is highly important for the student to take special note of the *ultimate* results stemming from any conscious lack of planning. To fully appreciate this, the author returned after a weekend in the country to interview Stu concerning the eventual outcome of the decisions he had made during the one-hour marathon. The results were as follows:

The short circuit which caused the coffeepot not to work saved a possible fire when it was discovered by the electrical contractor that the wrong wiring had been installed in the trailer. Thus, because of Stu's plugging in the coffeepot, he saved having to purchase a new trailer.

The pump "demonstration" took care of the water and saved having to buy a pump. Years later, the plumbing contractor secured a very profitable job replacing the pipe in the men's room. The lobby

45

safe attracted lots of visitors and discouraged crooks who preferred to work in the dark. The President loved his vault office since it ideally fit his hobby—which happened to be mushroom growing. Stu's cement Cadillac worked well as a drainage system and Stu was very happy with his new Cadillac and the redhead.

Thus, you see the real finesse required for proper application of Calculated Reactionism. The practitioner must totally avoid all planning, but be extremely agile in his reactions.

In summary, Calculated Reactionism is most often effective as a short-range strategy. The ability to react quickly is essential and these reactions should set you up as a creative action-oriented individual.

Calculated Reactionism calls for a high degree of creativity which enables you to respond to problems in such a way that the eventual outcome is as good or better than one developed through careful planning.

It has been found that this strategy works best with small companies or middle managers on the way up in large companies. When applying Calculated Reactionism, it is extremely important to publicize the *results* of the outcomes, not the *causes* of the problems. This way, top management will usually regard the Calculated Reactionistic planner as a "real fireball, action-oriented tiger on the way up," and all those other descriptive phrases applied to future recipients of the key to the executive washroom.

# 6: PROLIFIC PONDEROUSNESS

THE PLANNING STRAT-
egy of Prolific Ponderousness is often thought of as
being the direct opposite of Calculated Reactionism.
Its importance as an Obstructive Planning Technique makes it very special, since it is growing at a
rapidly accelerating rate. More and more businesses,
civic governments, and universities are recognizing
the value of Prolific Ponderousness.

When attempting to communicate the full importance of this technique, it is not sufficient to
merely state that Prolific Ponderousness is the *presence* of too much planning. This might lead students
to believe that they can accomplish Prolific Ponderousness solely through continuous planning. While
this may be true in some cases, skillful obstructive
managers employ subtle nuances which help ac-
count for this strategy's rapid growth as a major
Obstructive Planning Technique.

47

Another factor that contributes greatly to its widespread acceptance is the very culture of our society which reveres planning, placing it second only to motherhood. Planning spans literally all aspects of our life, from planned parenthood on through to planned interment. Thus, because this Obstructive Technique requires infinite planning and replanning, it is not difficult to understand the wide popularity of Prolific Ponderousness in business circles.

As with the techniques previously discussed, it is highly important to understand: first, the objectives of using the technique; second, the conditions under which it is most effective; third, the most appropriate method of application; and fourth, its potential results.

Let's now examine each of these points prior to reviewing an actual case.

## OBJECTIVE

Three major objectives can be accomplished through proper implementation of Prolific Ponderousness. The first of these is to delay making a decision which obviously needs to be made. The need to make a decision occurs only too often in business, government, and academic life. It is easily understandable, since anyone in a leadership capacity is frequently expected by his subordinates (or his superiors) to make decisions. However, it behooves an experienced obstructive manager to postpone this painful decision point as long as possible. This is most certainly true if he himself is in any way threatened by the outcome of the decision that he must make. Thus, a prime objective for using Prolific Ponderousness is to delay a decision.

The second objective which often can be accomplished through proper application of this technique is to stall for time and gain credibility as a cover for a total ineptness to perform as expected. If an obstructive manager has conscientiously applied himself, eventually he will reach a position, via a promotion or other course of events, which he is totally unqualified to carry out. At this point, he needs some technique which will disguise his ineptness and give him the opportunity to either learn what is required of him, or work toward a further promotion into a different area. Using Prolific Ponderousness toward this objective can be very advantageous since it is a great consumer of time.

The third objective which fits quite well with this technique is to create jobs and reduce efficiency to an acceptable level. The need for job proliferation and the caution to be wary of the overly efficient organization have been discussed in previous chapters as a valued approach in obstructive management. Thus, the application of Prolific Ponderousness in creating additional jobs or reducing a dangerously high degree of efficiency to a more acceptable level is certainly commendable.

## OPTIMUM CONDITIONS

To illustrate the optimum conditions under which Prolific Ponderousness can be applied, one can look to almost any field of endeavor. For example, a small-town politician who as an elected official must either delay a decision or be voted out of office, could find great solace in the proper application of this Obstructive Technique.

Another example—which should be obvious to the adept student—is that of the high-level executive who has been promoted to a new position and needs time to solidify his situation. His application of this planning principle would allow him to establish a reputation as a valued planner, while in essence he is merely stalling for time.

In the academic world, the President or Provost of a university could use Prolific Ponderousness to justify adding facilities or faculty to his staff. A new university Planning Department, complete with an exotic computerized facility, can do wonders toward slowing down the efficiency of the overall organization while giving the impression of forward-thinking management.

From the whole spectrum of business and civic life, these are only three examples of what could be considered optimum conditions for implementation of Prolific Ponderousness. The technique fits so well into the contemporary environment that it is extremely difficult to even state the optimum conditions, since nearly any set of circumstances can be used as a potential for application of this principle.

## METHODS OF APPLICATION

How to apply this technique is largely dependent on the whims of the initiator. Although his status and power within the organization can facilitate his choice of some of the more sophisticated methods, status and prestige are not limiting factors in themselves. Numerous low- and middle-level managers have effectively utilized Prolific Ponderousness.

The more notable successful applications of this principle have involved the use of one or more of the following vehicles to plan and replan: research studies, feasibility studies, strategic planning groups, study teams, task forces, and computer applications such as regression analysis and linear programming. While any one of these approaches can be effective on its own, used in consort they can serve to delay a decision almost indefinitely.

A research study, for example, is a most appropriate obstructive device when used by the initiator to determine whether anything should be done differently by an organization or within an organization. Basically, what a research study can attempt to do is determine what potentials exist within an organization to accomplish tasks no one else has ever thought of doing. Generally, a research study is

51

best carried out by an external organization or consulting group who can use this task as a means of justifying its own existence and setting itself up for further assignments.

A feasibility study determines whether a potential function or change in direction will work once it is instituted. This type of study's main value is that it can be structured to examine an infinite number of contingencies. The feasibilities can be studied indefinitely, thus delaying any chance of a conclusion or decision.

The introduction of strategic or long-range planning into an organization may not seem superficially to be the obstructive objective. When it is properly implemented down to the lowest level of an organization, however, the individual worker may devote so much time to planning that there is no time left for actually accomplishing the work, thereby fulfilling the objective of this technique.

Study teams and task forces also have similar fringe benefits; if properly structured and charged with a complex mission, the participants will have to devote so much time to their task-force activities that their own organizational responsibilities will be almost totally abandoned, thus causing even more organizational confusion. But actually, study teams and task forces are fairly recent innovations in the search for better tools in Obstructive Management. Their true value lies in the manner in which they are constructed. Both are usually formed and directed to submit a report which will either agree with higher management and reinforce a preconceived idea, or to spend countless hours examining a proposal which management has no intention whatsoever of implementing.

To insure their proper ineffectiveness, it is highly important study teams and task forces be structured in such a way that the individual members have nothing in common. Better still, they should dislike each other heartily and have such narrow specialities that they cannot even talk to each other. This is currently termed a multidiscipline team whose members are composed from both horizontal and vertical slices of any organization. An ideal team might be composed of the comptroller, the company psychologist, an outside physicist, and the janitor.

Computer applications used in the planning process are one of the most valuable assets to Prolific Ponderousness. A properly written computer program can study alternatives almost indefinitely. Also, if whatever decision finally emerges is unsatisfactory, the programmer can readily be blamed without endangering the security of any of the parties who originally requested the model be created.

In short, the executive who wishes to apply Prolific Ponderousness has at his fingertips a vast array of tools and methods. He only has to choose an appropriate subject and then create a team or introduce one of the approaches to be well on his way toward application of this Obstructive Technique. A key point to remember is that this total arsenal of tools is available. If one method does not accomplish the objective, another can be quickly employed to further delay the eventual decision.

## POTENTIAL RESULTS

While we have previously explored the objectives for using this technique, it is quite essential to understand some of the potential results that can accrue to the obstructive manager. The first result which definitely is within the realm of feasibility is further promotion due to the innovative approach he has taken in introducing advanced planning. It is important to note that it is not at all necessary for him to have any of his plans *actually* adopted or put into action. Just the mere fact that he has done the planning is a great indicator of his future capabilities as a manager.

A second result to realistically expect is that through proper application of this principle it is relatively easy to increase the operating costs of any department or business and to lower the total efficiency of the organization, provided this entire concept is properly carried down to the lowest operating level. To reap the potential benefits, the obstructive manager must, "make planning a way of life" and insure that everyone, regardless of their level in the organization, spend a major portion of their time designing magnificent plans for future operations which never quite take place.

It is possible for managers to almost totally abdicate the decision-making responsibility, because even if the manager is forced to reach a decision, he can always turn around and blame it on the output of some task force, study team, or research that has been done on the subject. The true master of this technique hardly ever reaches the point of having to make a decision.

With this new understanding, it is time to review a case study.

The refuse-disposal situation in Tackey Acres, New Jersey, had grown to critical proportions. Previous town administrations had employed a highly effective system of refuse disposal: They buried it. They had received acclaim through the creation of such recreation aids as Seedy Hills Country Club and Beer Can Marina, both of which had become favored recreation sites over the years. The problem facing Tackey Acres was that there was no more available space on which to deposit trash, and therefore something had to be done.

Into the political furor entered Wentworth Deshevell, who tossed his garbage can lid into the ring in the race for First Selectman. The Deshevell campaign got off to a flying start with ecologists taking pictures of Wentworth Deshevell driving a rusting tomato can down the fourth fairway at Seedy Hills and proclaiming loudly, "Landfill is not the answer! Tackey Acres needs systematic long-range refuse planning!"

The word planning wove its magic spell despite the fact that for years Tackey Acres had had a Town

Planner and a Planning and Zoning Committee. The concept of new plans was highly intriguing to the voters. They had had their fill of landfill and were looking for new modern ways of refuse disposal. Thus, First Selectman Deshevell was elected by a landslide, as a rebuff to landfill.

One of his first acts in office was to close the landfill operation and announce to the private garbage collectors that they would have to take their garbage elsewhere. The only "elsewhere" they could find was, of course, the neighboring towns, who were not terribly thrilled to receive Tackey Acres' trash. But nevertheless, this was the edict handed down by Deshevell.

His next act was to establish a new Office of Ecological Planning and offer contracts for study teams to examine the situation. The scent of profits in Tackey Acres was appealing despite the abundance of other competing aromas, and literally dozens of firms rushed to bid on the formation of study teams to examine the trash-disposal problems. Finally, two firms were selected who dutifully went about the task of developing a long-range study.

The study effort followed a classic course starting with basic research on what to do with garbage in very broad terms, to be followed by a feasibility study to determine whether any of the ideas uncovered through research were indeed practical, and then finally resulting in the strategic plan to provide for long-range refuse disposal.

The study teams and task forces worked diligently throughout most of Selectman Deshevell's first term in office. Glowing reports of their progress were printed monthly in the town papers for the citizenry to enjoy.

Then, without warning, a major crisis arose. The neighboring towns were getting literally fed up with Tackey Acres' trash, and refused to take any more from the garbage collectors. Selectman Deshevell had reached a decision point. Because he was nearing the end of his first term and facing an upcoming election, he was forced to take action.

The action he took astounded everyone, for it seemed to be the most unlikely of all possible solutions. In one of the early research studies conducted by a task force, the comment had been that the terrain around Tackey Acres was dull and uninteresting, lacking graceful hills or distinctive landmarks. This remark caught the imagination of Selectman Deshevell, and he ordered the independent trash collectors to start depositing all of the rubbish behind the Town Hall and to build a mountain for Tackey Acres.

The newspapers were full of artists' renditions of the beautiful mountain that was growing rapidly behind the Town Hall. The papers were also careful to state that this was an innovative temporary solution pending final completion of the study teams' and task forces' efforts toward developing a permanent solution.

With the election just days away, Selectman Deshevell held an important news conference at which time he hinted that a sophisticated computer model was being built under his direction to study the long-range refuse disposal system. This romance of a computer model carried Deshevell over the top. The day after the election, re-elected Selectman Wentworth Deshevell proudly dedicated Deshevell Mountain as a monument for the generations to come.

This brief case illustrates the real power of Prolific Ponderousness and the aura of efficiency which surrounds the very concept of planning. Handled properly, the obstructive manager can reap many benefits from proper application of this planning principle.

# II

## ORGANIZING

# 7: DEMOCRATIC FAVORITISM

WITH THE PLANNING
done, the next major managerial function to focus
on is organization. Whether organizing a complex
corporation or a Little League team, the method one
employs in establishing reporting relationships can
have a tremendous impact on overall efficiency.

The structures illustrated in this and following
chapters are designed to insure further implementation of whatever Obstructive Planning Techniques
have been selected. In short, once you have laid the
plans to foul up an organization, you must organize
properly to accomplish this objective.

The concepts to be presented here have been applied at various organizational levels. While quite
some emphasis is placed on organizational structure
in order to illustrate the value of misplaced reporting
relationships, the main thrust of this and the following chapters is toward organizational *climate*.

The student should approach organization with a positive attitude, recognizing that with the knowledge to be gained from this technique and others which are discussed later, he will invariably be able to design the most inappropriate organization for any given enterprise.

The study of organizations has been legitimized and classified as hierarchiology by Dr. Laurence J. Peter in *The Peter Principle*. It involves the various methods and designs employed in charting reporting relationships. To aid the student, some of the more significant charts are illustrated for further study.

When selecting an organizational structure, it is important to remember that the type of organization must reflect and harmonize with the ambitions of the obstructionist manager. This makes the whole concept of reporting relationships highly critical.

Democratic Favoritism is one of the more popular organizational styles because it is easily installed and adapts directly to the ambitions of the leader. But another reason for its popularity is the connotation of the word democratic in its title. While this implies that everyone is equal, that the same weight is given in decision-making situations, that all votes count, the student will soon learn that some votes count more than others. However, Democratic Favoritism makes all the people within an organization feel that they share equally, and that the organization is really trying to avoid a pyramidal type of structure.

In establishing Democratic Favoritism, a frequent

approach is to carefully analyze an existing organization and then reorganize, establishing reporting relationships that will completely stifle initiative. This can be accomplished by re-assigning functional managers whose prime experience and interests lie outside the areas they are to supervise.

Another way to implement this principle is to build a formal organization with well-established reporting relationships, and then superimpose on it an informal covert organization which represents the true power structure. In both instances, it is of prime importance to identify and cultivate individuals who are either patently ineffective or who have some common bond linking them together. These individuals will become the functional managers in the formal organization and the covert leaders in the informal organization.

Fortunately for the student, there is a classic case to illustrate this prime organizational principle. It is unique in that the company's founder structured it from the very start to function under a Democratic Favoritism organizational approach. This case involves the Doddering Equipment Works, Limited. The principal is Colonel Reginald D. Doddering, the founder of the company.

Colonel Doddering was born in London in 1892. He attended Oxford and served with distinction in Her Majesty's Royal Artillery during several wars. After World War II, he founded Doddering Equipment Works, Limited.

Being a highly creative individual, one of his first

thoughts toward setting up his new organization was to invent a slogan which would indicate or reflect its policy toward business. Colonel Doddering was fascinated by initials, so his slogan evolved by taking the first letters of each of the words in his company—D.E.W.—which much to his delight spelled the word dew. From this, he developed his slogan—"D.E.W. unto others before they DO unto you."

With the idea for a company and a slogan for it to operate under, he needed a vital organization to carry out his objectives.

Reginald's Oxford schooling and army training had conditioned him to accept the vertical pyramid type of organizational structure. Having lived under such a hierarchy most of his life, now, as the head of his own company, he wished to create a form of organization which would be quite different. Having majored in history in addition to military science and tactics, the concept of a democracy fascinated him. Thoughts of all of the chaps working together, shoulder to the wheel, all equal, simply enthralled him.

Naturally, he would lead the organization and he would have some good lieutenant types to keep an eye on things, but they all would be equal.

The Colonel's first move was to discard all titles within the organization and replace them with the term, "Associate." He established an Associate for Marketing, an Associate for Finance, an Associate for Personnel, and an Associate for Manufacturing.

With this group of titles firmly established, Colonel Doddering set about selecting individuals to fill these posts. He realized that even in a democracy you really must have *some* leadership expertise, and, of course, the best leaders he knew were his friends in the army. Thus, his selection process for filling the top openings in the company was to go to the Retired Officers' Association and recruit four of his closest friends, three of whom just happened to be relatives.

Reginald then set about to build the next layer of his organization. The selection process used here was to search for Associates who had recently graduated from Oxford and showed some promise in such fields as sales, accounting, engineering, employment, and training.

To keep his democracy flourishing, this group of younger Associates were given the titles of "Assistant to." Thus, they became Associate Assistants to the Associates for Marketing, Finance, Personnel, and Manufacturing.

After Reginald's next move—establishing a firm policy of promotion only from within—he then recognized that he needed some people to do the actual work in the organization. His prime experience of having been in the army immediately led him to hiring a group of retired foot soldiers to become Associate Workers, such as salesmen, clerks, draftsmen, interviewers, and trainers. Reginald rationalized that by using all retired army foot soldiers as workers, he could eliminate any chance of unionization since everyone was on a pension and wages were not all that important.

With his new organization in place, Reginald held frequent staff meetings with his first two layers of Associates. All the Associates were invited, but somehow the Associate Workers never seemed to have the time to attend.

To further integrate his democratic organization, Reginald formed various multidiscipline teams to work on conceptual problems. These teams were composed of some "Associate Assistants to" and at least one of the key Associates. Reginald realized that even though they were all equal, some were, in the words of George Orwell, "more equal than others." The Associate Workers were invited to join these multidiscipline teams, but somehow they never seemed to be available.

The absence of the Associate Workers was discussed often at staff meetings where the key Associates were most vocal claiming that the Associate Workers just do not appreciate the opportunities a democracy offers. Reginald agreed heartily with this, since in his eyes everyone shares an equal responsibility for the success of the organization, and therefore should participate.

The multidiscipline teams were used extensively to review proposals emanating from Assistants to Associates. Special care was taken that the Associate for Manufacturing and the Associate for Finance were members of any team reviewing creative proposals originating from Assistants to Associates in the Marketing or Personnel areas. This served to keep the organization with its eye on the target, all working together without any interference of any harebrained ideas. In fact, it was not long before the flow of creative proposals emanating from Marketing and Personnel just dried up.

Reginald was extremely happy to have created a truly democratic organization. His associates dressed alike, thought alike, and in his eyes, even started to look alike. Certainly, Reginald had his favorites, but they were democratic favorites.

This then is how the organization concept of Democratic Favoritism was formed at Doddering Equipment Works. In Reginald's mind, he had eliminated the traditional pyramidal type of organization and created a new model for hierarchiologists to wonder over. Shown, in Figure 1, is a diagram of Reginald's organizational structure.

To assist students of Obstructive Management in identifying the existence of Democratic Favoritism in their own organizations, the author worked with Colonel Doddering and designed the following short test. If the questions are answered honestly, this quiz can pinpoint the existence of Democratic Favoritism in any organization. To take the test, just answer "Yes" or "No" in response to each of the questions listed below.

1. Do creative departments report to technically-oriented managers?

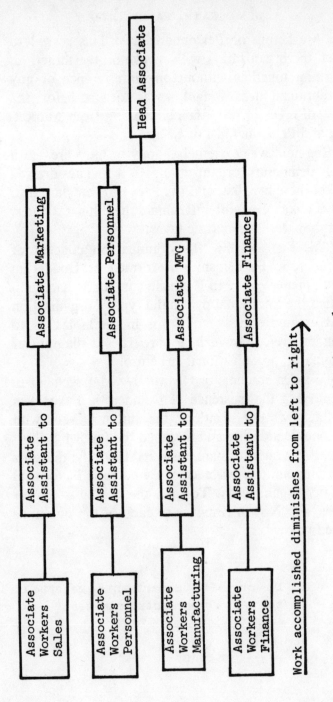

Figure 1:
DODDERING'S CONCEPTUAL HORIZONTAL
ORGANIZATION FOR DEMOCRATIC FAVORITISM

2. Are certain individuals more vocal at staff meetings than others?

3. Have you been told that "everyone shares an equal responsibility"?

4. Have more than four company managers attended the same university?

5. Have Administrative Assistants been added at various levels?

6. Are all workers referred to as "Associates"?

7. Are proposals reviewed by "Multidisciplined Teams"?

8. Do certain managers and subordinates seem to dress alike?

9. Has there been a long-standing policy of promotion always from within?

10. Are relatives allowed on the payroll?

To score this test, simply add up the number of "Yes" and "No" responses. Each "Yes" answer counts ten percent; thus, six "Yes" answers would indicate a sixty percent probability that Democratic Favoritism in one form or another is being practiced.

In summary, then, if you are setting up an organization and wish to establish the concept of Democratic Favoritism, you now know how it should be approached. If, on the other hand, you find yourself in a company where this organizational principle is already in practice, your best approach is to strive to become slightly more equal than others.

# 8: FLEXIBLE RIGIDITY

IN CHAPTER SEVEN, IT was stressed that the concept of Democratic Favoritism could best be employed at creation of a new organization. In this chapter, we will examine an obstructive technique used most often to maintain the status quo within a mature organization.

In this day and age of constant change, where the only predictable variable is change itself, it is comforting for the obstructive manager to have at his command a technique which will guarantee that things will keep running the way they always have. The concept of Flexible Rigidity is founded upon the premise that all groups have the right to establish their own structures, provided that they conform to pre-established organizational norms. In this definition lies the true value of the concept, since it supposedly allows total flexibility in reorganizing a department or a group, but places the restriction that such organizations must conform to existing organizational patterns.

"Flexible Rigidity," one learned scholar has said, "is an organizational principle which recognizes that maintaining the structure is far more important than the work being performed." This definition seems to shed even more light on the significance of this most important obstructive concept. Organizations all over the country are faced almost monthly with opportunities to enter new ventures that would require organizational change. However, by adhering to the principle of Flexible Rigidity, these opportunities are passed up and the archaic structure is preserved since it does indeed seem to be more important than the work being performed.

Opportunities for the application of Flexible Rigidity can be found generally in organizations that have acquired some history or tradition due to their having been in a particular industry or business for a number of years. Newer organizations are constantly in a state of flux and have not really established working relationships and organizational patterns; thus, they are the least likely to adopt this principle. The concept becomes viable only when a manager can truly make the statement, "That's the way we do it and that's the way we have *always* done it here at good old Company X." Without tradition, this concept is almost useless.

The major value of Flexible Rigidity is its application as a device to stifle the creativity of subordinate managers. It is particularly useful whenever a new subordinate manager is brought in from the outside through some quirk in the recruiting policy. Outsiders, who have not been steeped in the traditions, have the annoying habit of attempting to change parts of the organization and improve the quality of the work being performed. This immediately places higher management in a defensive role. Without the concept of Flexible Rigidity to fall back on at such times, higher management would have no valid defense against change.

To apply this principle properly in an established organization, a manager who is faced with or threatened by an outsider desiring to change his organization seemingly delegates total authority and flexibility to do whatever the new manager feels is important. This delegation is often accompanied by statements stressing the importance of new thinking, new ideas, and new work concepts. The outsider is encouraged to "look around" and come up with some plan for his department or group. This covers the flexible part of the concept, or the apparent willingness to accept organizational change.

The next part of this concept involves rigidity in accepting any proposed organizational changes. To accomplish this, top management must have firmly established policies governing all of the following areas:

73

| | |
|---|---|
| *Head count* | *Reporting* |
| *Job title* | *relationships* |
| *Work flow* | *Work measure-* |
| *process* | *ment criteria* |
| *Working* | *Working hours* |
| *conditions* | *Dress code* |
| *Job description* | *Salary grade* |

Now to the student, this list may seem so completely restrictive that one might wonder why any manager in his right mind would accept a position to work under these constraints. This is a perfectly valid question. However, the techniques of implementing Flexible Rigidity call for extreme adroitness so that all of these constraints do not become apparent at once. Thus, you have the situation where the new manager is blithely working toward a proposal to reorganize, totally unaware of this list of rigid policies which have been in existence over a long period of time.

The true value of these constraints actually lies in the very vagueness of their origin. In most organizations, it is virtually impossible to identify individuals who established the original policy. If ever questioned as to why a certain constraint exists, it is perfectly appropriate and proper to answer, "That is the way we have always done it."

For the student to fully appreciate the finesse required in implementing Flexible Rigidity, the author spent a considerable amount of time observing and recording the following conversations. The time frames covered by these discussions are extremely important, since they indicate the pace necessary to apply this concept effectively. Reproduced here in detail are the series of meetings held over an extended period of time between a senior obstructive manager applying Flexible Rigidity and his newly recruited subordinate department manager who has been brought in from the outside.

| | |
|---|---|
| SENIOR MANAGER: | Well, it's certainly nice to have you on board at last. We are looking for great things to come out of your department now that you are with us. You have an excellent background, and I am sure you are full of new ideas to get us really cracking. What I want you to do is to take your time. Look around and see what's happening. Come up with fresh, new thinking, new ideas, new work concepts. We've been doing the same thing too long and are anxious for a change. |
| SUBORDINATE MANAGER: | Thanks boss. I'm really looking forward to working with you. I've had lots of experience in this field, and really am ready to try out some new thinking, ideas I first thought of back |

with my old company, but never had the chance to apply. I'll do exactly as you suggest, and take a little time. I'll be back to you with my plan very soon.

(*One month later.*)

SENIOR MANAGER: I know you've been trying to get to me, but I've been pretty tied up with customer golf dates. Well, what do you think about our organization now?

SUBORDINATE MANAGER: Boss, I have been giving it a lot of thought. I think I have come up with some ideas that I can implement almost immediately which will improve the work flow process in my department.

SENIOR MANAGER: Great, let's hear about it.

SUBORDINATE MANAGER: Well, the way the work is set up now, every bit of work done is checked four times by four different individuals before it leaves the department. I would like to segment the work so that one individual has total

76

responsibility for a job. That way, each of my people will feel a true responsibility for completing whatever work he has to do.

SENIOR
MANAGER:

Hmmmmmmm. Sounds very interesting. However, this system was carefully thought out a number of years ago, and the decision was made that if we had one person assigned to doing a complete job and he leaves, we are liable to lose the total expertise. Also, as you know, people do make mistakes. Therefore, if everyone in the department works on every single job doing just a small piece of it, it gets checked and rechecked so we know it is accurate when it leaves the department. I think maybe you'd better just leave the work flow process the way it is.

Golly, I'm going to have to cut this just a little short. I am due at the country club in thirty minutes. Come back and we'll get together a little later, after you've had a chance to come up with other ideas and

77

develop them a little further. See you later.


(*Two months later.*)

| | |
|---|---|
| SENIOR MANAGER: | Glad we could get together again. I'm sure by now you must be champing at the bit to implement some of your new ideas. |
| SUBORDINATE MANAGER: | Boy, I sure am. I've been giving this a lot of thought and by just adding two people to my organization I can improve the work output by as much as seventy-five percent. |
| SENIOR MANAGER: | Hmmmmmmmm. Sounds very interesting. |
| SUBORDINATE MANAGER: | Yes, simply by changing the methods we use for measuring the work produced, stressing more qualitative approaches rather than quantitative, and with the addition of just two people, I can upgrade the entire output and be really responsive in terms of servicing the other departments who depend upon me. |

SENIOR
MANAGER:

You know, a lot of time was spent a few years back establishing our policy of head count. It seems to me that this idea of yours just might be exceeding that head count by a considerable amount. At the time your department was originally established, it was determined that the work could be handled successfully with the number of people you are now authorized to have. Also, the work measurement criteria that we use has given us a pretty good indication of each individual's work. I really would hate to see that change, since we might not have the real feel we have now for each individual's value to the organization. Why don't we think about this a while and uh, let's get together again in the real near future.

(*Four months later.*)

SENIOR
MANAGER:

Boy, we've both been so busy we just never got back together. But I am really anxious to hear how things are going in your department.

SUBORDINATE MANAGER: Well, I am making some progress, but I would like to talk to you today about a couple of things that I really think will make a tremendous difference. First of all, there has been a lot of work done in behavioral science about job enrichment, and I would like to apply it within my department, starting out by changing some of the titles of the people to make them think the work they're doing is more important—and having each one re-do his own job description so that it is more relevant in terms of the work he is actually performing. I looked over the old job descriptions and they literally haven't been changed in the last ten years. My people are doing totally different kinds of work today.

SENIOR MANAGER: Hmmmmmmm. Job enrichment, eh? Well, I guess whatever you do internally in your own department can't hurt, if

you think your people would
be happy calling each other by
different titles. Okay, I can't
see any problems there. If you
want to write up little job
descriptions you just use internally within your own department that they can keep in their
desks and look at, that might
be all right too. But you know,
we might have a problem with
some of the other departments.
We just can't have all the departments rewriting their job
descriptions because, you
know, a job description and a
worker's title are very important in our salary administration and the establishment of
our salary grades. We pay our
employees very well. These
salary grades have been set up
for a number of years now,
and ah—well, I would hate to
see anything that might disrupt
payroll. So if you want to use
your titles and job descriptions
in your own department, fine,
that's okay, but let's just don't
send them on to personnel.
Let's leave it the way it is so

we won't disrupt the other operating departments. I'll, uh, get back to you on some of your other ideas. Thanks for stopping by.

(*Five months later.*)

SENIOR
MANAGER:

Well, we never seem to get time to sit down and talk about your new ideas. What did you come up with this time?

SUBORDINATE
MANAGER:

You know, boss, I have been doing a lot of thinking about some of the conditions my people have to work under and the requirements that seem to have been established for the dress code—of what they wear during their work. Well, some of my guys have to get out into the field and do some pretty heavy work occasionally, and also talk with people who are in sport clothes and casual attire, and these darn blue suits with white shirts and black ties are kind of restrictive, make you stand out. I would like to sort of relax the dress code in my department and change some of the working conditions —bring in some new lighting and do away with some of these big old desks that aren't really necessary in their offices. They hardly have room to move. I would like to get some good work tables and comfortable chairs for them to sit in and talk with their peers so we can establish a little better working conditions for them.

SENIOR MANAGER: Hmmmmmmm. Sounds like you may have a little bit of a problem there. Uh, you know this company has been in business for a number of years and you know it has almost become a tradition to have our people all dress alike—that way you can spot one of them on a job. We know he is one of our guys, not one of the competitors who slouch around in casual attire. I kind of think that might disrupt our whole organization, and certainly I don't see how it would improve the efficiency.

Better leave the dress code alone for now, and as far as the working conditions are concerned, we had a group in here, oh gosh, it must have been twenty years ago, that looked at our office requirements. Those desks that you are speaking of were designed by our founder who liked that sort of desk. Mine is a little different because I have a little different level job than you, but we each have a set so that each level has the desks, the equipment, and the materials they need to do the job at that level. As they progress, of course, offices change, and this is the incentive. If we changed it all below, there would really be no incentive to get ahead. I think maybe we better not disrupt the organization by changing your operation. Then everybody else would want it, and, gosh, the company just couldn't afford it. Well, we will talk a bit more on this a little later on, but for now let's just not do anything in that area.

*(Six months later.)*

| | |
|---|---|
| SENIOR MANAGER: | Well, I just don't get to see enough of you. It's a shame we can't get more creative ideas out of your department, but I have just not had the time to sit down and talk with you about it. These customer golf matches are getting heavier all the time. |
| SUBORDINATE MANAGER: | Well, boss, I have two problems on my mind today. One is that the people we are dealing with outside of my department just don't seem to work the same hours that my department does. Our customers have different working hours, and I don't see how we can be totally responsive to their needs by working the same shift that all of the other people work in the plant. I would like to install a more flexible working time for our people so that they can come in when they know they will be able to reach our customers. |
| SENIOR MANAGER: | Hmmmmmmm. Interesting thought. However, you know |

85

down over the years our customers have gotten to know that our switchboard and our people are at their desks at fixed hours of the day. Now, if we were to change that drastically, some of our old-time customers might get upset, and I wouldn't want to risk that, you know. We have a tradition here that we are Johnny-on-the-spot at 8:00 in the morning and that we close down at 5:00 sharp. I think that if we tried to vary these hours, we might get into some real problems and also upset some of the other departments who would see us coming in at different times of the day. It really doesn't sound as if that one would work too well.

SUBORDINATE MANAGER: Well, maybe you're right. One final thing, boss. I think that my department really would function better if it were reporting up through operations rather than through a staff department. No offense against you, boss, you have been pretty good to me, but we just don't seem to be responsive to the needs of the operational end of the business. Therefore, I would like to propose that my whole department be moved over to report to operations.

SENIOR
MANAGER:       Hmmmmmmm. We had a look at that a number of years back. When the organization was set up, we called in some outside consultants to look us over. Based on their evaluation, it has been pretty much tradition to have your department reporting to a staff function. Operations guys are really doing a different thing. However, I will take that one under advisement a little bit, and I will get back to you soon.


(*Three months later.*)


SENIOR
MANAGER:       Well, sorry to hear that you are leaving. Thought you were going to do some really great things for us, but I guess you

can't turn down that job offer you had from outside. We will miss you around here. You were full of great ideas and great innovations. Good luck and let's keep in touch over the years.

SUBORDINATE MANAGER: Thanks, boss. I really think this might be an opportunity for me to move on and take my ideas and really make a go of them with this new organization. So long for now, boss. I'll keep in touch.

After the subordinate manager leaves, the senior manager thinks to himself, "Well, he really wasn't our type of guy. He couldn't adopt our type of organization or our traditions. He really will be better off in another organization."

This dialogue, spanning a number of months, illustrates beautifully the finesse required to apply Flexible Rigidity. Every opportunity was given the subordinate manager to think creatively and independently toward reorganization. But in each case, whatever was proposed came into conflict with an established policy. This caused the subordinate to eventually become dissatisfied with his position and quit the company. Now the senior manager is no longer threatened and can quite logically suggest to personnel that they never bring in another outsider since he simply won't understand the traditions of the company. Thus, for the obstructive manager working in a tradition-laden company, Flexible Rigidity is the best technique to use to preserve the status quo. Its effectiveness can be seen dramatically from the following graph (Figure 2).

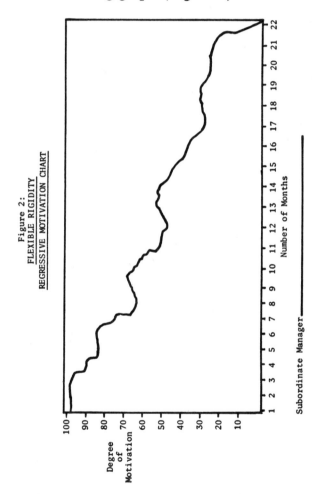

Figure 2:
FLEXIBLE RIGIDITY
REGRESSIVE MOTIVATION CHART

# 9: CONCENTRATED DECENTRALIZATION

PROTECTION AGAINST
over-efficiency is a common need among obstructive managers. This also holds true for entire organizations in today's rapidly growing marketplace. A parent organization lives in fear of becoming unnecessary to the successful operation of one or more of its components. To respond to this overpowering need for inefficiency, the concept of Concentrated Decentralization came into being. It is an obstructive organizational principle in which the decision power appears to be located in decentralized units, but is in fact highly concentrated within a centralized headquarters. The end result that can be expected from proper application of this technique is a form of reverse-synergy where the sum of all of the parts becomes less than the whole headquarters.

One of the greatest benefits of Concentrated Decentralization is its flexibility in terms of when it should be applied. For example, it fits very logically into an acquisition program if the headquarters staff feels that the ultimate success of the newly acquired enterprise could conceivably threaten the parent company. It can also be used very effectively prior to the divestment of a successful business so that the parent company can take credit for its success. Finally, it is most useful at the beginning of any new venture from within the company to insure its eventual collapse.

While literally any manager can initiate the implementation phase of Concentrated Decentralization, this generally falls to some corporate staff function. In reviewing many of the cases that have been recorded, the Finance Department or Comptroller's Office seems to be the prime initiator. This is not too difficult to understand, since financial personnel are the first ones to view enviously a successful balance sheet of a profitable component and decide to get in on the action. After all, independent success could reflect unfavorably upon corporate finance. Thus, the immediate application of Concentrated Decentralization becomes necessary, and they move in quickly with a long list of financial control systems, in-depth analyses of accounting procedures, and cost audits which will surely strangle the decentralized operation.

Once a successful unit or component has been identified, the personnel people descend with career pathing plans which lead talent away from the successful operation, salary administration practices to take away pay benefits, job and man specifications to firmly establish mediocrity, and reams of paperwork to set up management by objectives, performance evaluation, and career counseling. All of these moves are aimed at totally stifling the creativity of the individual component.

Other corporate staffs arrive with standardization of data communications, market-research activity reports, product development and planning procedures, manufacturing audits, engineering studies, and the integration of marketing services such as advertising, promotion, strategic planning, and so forth.

In some of the more successfully decimated companies, practitioners of Concentrated Decentralization have even managed to pressure a successful sales component into taking on a totally nonrelated product line that is of no use at all to the market currently being served.

For the Obstructive Management student, such practices may seem rash and counter-productive. However, placed in a corporate-level assignment and forced to view the success of a decentralized component, it could become a matter of survival for the obstructive manager to either diminish the degree of success or attempt in some way to take credit for it. Thus, the concept of Concentrated Decentralization was born and came into frequent practice.

# APPLICATION

The student should not be misled into thinking that it is necessary to be located in the Finance Department or wait for the Finance Department to make the first move. Admittedly, it is difficult to get the jump on financial managers in the application of Concentrated Decentralization. They usually are the ones to get the first inkling of impending success within a decentralized unit. However, an obstructive Personnel Manager, Marketing Manager, or Manufacturing Manager can equally well start the process.

The first step is to recognize the apparent danger and set objectives which will grow out of proper application of the principle. For example, a well-trained obstructive Personnel Manager, viewing with alarm the reduced turnover rate existing in a newly acquired unit, could set the objective: "With proper application of Concentrated Decentralization involving the standardization of hiring practices, turnovers should increase by fifteen percent." Now it becomes quite possible and practical to measure the results.

With the objective firmly established, the next step is to "sell the concept" of standardization to higher management. This rarely ever presents much of a problem. Top management succumbs quite easily to proposals recommending tighter corporate controls as long as realistic-sounding benefits can be pointed to for each control.

Thus, it is recommended that the student spend time drawing up a benefit analysis chart patterned after the magnificently devious approach used by J. Philmore Potley, Vice-President of Personnel for Dulltronics, Inc.

J. P. P. designed the chart (see Figure 3) when he was attempting to beat out the Financial Vice-President of Dulltronics in a race to diminish the effectiveness of a newly acquired rapid-growth component.

Now on the surface, and certainly when viewed by Dulltronics' top management, this chart seems to present some highly attractive benefits. However, the astute obstructive manager would quickly ask the question, "Benefits from whose point of view?" The answer, on close scrutiny, is J. Philmore Potley's! To illustrate this, let's review each benefit from Potley's point of view:

1. *Ability to hire at corporate level for all components—reduction of extra recruiting costs.* (Potley's benefits: Larger corporate department, more stature. The only costs reduced will be those already covered by the components—now they will pay Potley.)

2. *One salary administration program reducing monitoring costs, improving morale.* (Reduces complaints from headquarters

# Figure 3
## J. P. P. BENEFIT ANALYSIS CHART

| ACTIVITY | BENEFIT |
|---|---|
| Standardized Selection Procedures | Ability to hire at corporate level for all components. Reduction of extra recruiting costs. |
| Standardized Job Descriptions | One salary administration program reducing monitoring costs, improving morale. |
| Centralized Training Facility | Continuity of training across all components means equal competence of managers, saves money. |
| Standardized Evaluation Program | Ability to transfer managers between components, since they will all be judged the same way, bringing flexibility and convenience. |
| Standardized Career Counseling | Ability to spot high-potential managers, better utilization of personnel, increased effectiveness. |
| Standardized Benefit Package | Promotes sense of belonging to corporation, eliminating unfair differentials, saving money. |

personnel who are making less than members of the new component. Improves Potley's morale.)

3. *Continuity of training across all components means equal competence of managers, savings of money.* (Overall inefficiency of training reduces threat to Potley. He also would save money by taking over the training facility owned by the new component.)

4. *Ability to transfer managers between components, since they will all be judged the same way, bringing flexibility and convenience.* (Now Potley can find homes for his ineffective friends and get them off his back.)

5. *Ability to spot high-potential managers, better utilization of personnel, increased effectiveness.* (Potley can spot potential trouble makers and boat-rockers and bury them before they become a problem, while increasing his effectiveness in the eyes of the President since he will not be compared with truly efficient managers.)

6. *Promotes sense of belonging to corporation, eliminating unfair differentials, sav-*

ORGANIZING

*ing money.* (Potley eliminates the unfair
differential between the poor package the
corporation is offering and the good one
presently offered in the component—saves
Potley embarrassment, saves Potley's budget money needed to increase headquarters' benefits.)

In review, the concept of Concentrated Decentralization is a valuable obstructive organizational principle used to smother the independence and growth
of a presently decentralized unit.

One case has recently come to light in which an
obstructive manager accomplished the almost un-
believable feat of employing an organizational
principle he termed Concentrated Centralized Decentralized Centralization. The facts are still somewhat obscure, but it appears that this genius
managed to completely dissolve a company through
application of this advanced concept.

As the story goes, he started in business as an
obscure obstructionist in the Financial Department
of a centralized corporation. From there, he con-
vinced management to spin off his department as a
separate unit. Next, he gained wide acclaim by jug-
gling the balance sheet, got promoted back into the
corporate office, and centralized the unit he had
spun off. The result was total collapse of the parent
company.

Since this organizational principle has not been
fully tested, it cannot be recommended to present

students of Obstructive Management. However, the very existence of such a case with its obvious nuances and implications should act as a stimulant and harbinger of things to come.

# 10: EXPEDITIOUS FILTERATION

SOME PURISTS FEEL
that the concept of Expeditious Filteration rightly
belongs under the section on controlling techniques.
However, since certain organizational structures are
required in order to properly institute Expeditious
Filteration, it seems to fit more aptly under the general heading of organizational principles. This is not
to say that this Obstructionist Technique cannot be
used as a controlling device once the sufficient organizational structure is in place. The concept of Expeditious Filteration holds that given a sufficient
number of layers in a hierarchy, meaningful information can no longer flow upward or downward.

This concept has its roots in a children's party
game. Five or more kids are lined up. The first one
is given a message to whisper into the second kid's
ear, he passes the message on to the third child, and

so forth down the line until the final child is asked to repeat his understanding of the message. Many hilarious results are obtained in terms of garbled messages.

Some of those children have long since grown up to become obstructive managers and now apply Expeditious Filteration up and down burgeoning hierarchies with much the same highly amusing results.

While on the surface this may appear to be an extremely simple concept to employ, it does take considerable adroitness to achieve a masterfully catastrophic result.

First of all, the obstructionist must determine if the organization, as it is now structured, has a sufficient number of layers to make the outcome worthwhile. Two or three layers are hardly enough to satisfy even the most novice obstructive managers. For really good results, most experienced practitioners demand at least five layers within the organization. Thus, a prime task facing anyone wishing to employ this technique is the creation of an appropriate organizational structure.

Fortunately, this rarely presents a problem in the average business organization. It is easily accomplished within any school system and has never even been considered as a problem in any governmental organization.

## DIRECT AND INDIRECT APPLICATIONS

There are two courses of action open to the obstructive manager wishing to apply this technique: the direct method, and the so-called indirect method.

The direct method can be effectively employed only if there are sufficient organizational layers beneath the practitioner or if he occupies a high position and can create additional needed organizational levels. This is the purist's form of Expeditious Filteration. Once given his own hierarchy, the obstructive manager can whisper commands into the ear of his next-in-command and be amused inmmediately when the lowest level in his organization attempts to carry out the garbled instructions.

The indirect method is one which is employed by staff department managers who do not have their own hierarchy and are forced to use someone else's. The results can be equally rewarding, however. To use the indirect method, a staff manager merely feeds information concerning a newly required report to the top manager in an existing hierarchy. After a reasonable waiting period of about one or two months, the results will flow back in an almost unrecognizable form.

Note that both the direct and indirect methods make use of the top-to-bottom approach; that is, the information originates at the top of a hierarchy and is fed downward for eventual implementation. A key point to remember is that instructions should be given in verbal form only, since written instructions can be accurately carried out sometimes. It is possible to employ Expeditious Filteration using a written format, but it is far more cumbersome, and the originator must take particular care in his choice of words to include as much ambiguity as possible and provide every opportunity for semantic difficulties.

Once the two basic approaches of direct and indirect top-to-bottom applications have been mastered and the ensuing obstructive results duly noted, it is suggested that the student attempt to employ the intermediate strategy of Bottom-Up Expeditious Filteration.

This variation can be initiated by a top manager or the corporate staff manager personally by visiting the lowest level of a multilayered hierarchy. During this visit, some idea for improved efficiency should be hinted at with the implication that if it is fed back upward it will receive serious consideration. Bottom-Up Expeditious Filteration produces even greater hilarity when it results in an organization-wide search by the company President to locate and fire the damn fool who came up with the idea.

Having mastered the intermediate strategies of Expeditious Filteration, the student then can move on to the most advanced version of this concept, which has come to be known as the Rebound, or Bouncing-Ball Gambit.

To accomplish this advanced strategy, the obstructive manager whispers a proposed plan into the ear of his next-in-command with the added instructions to *his* immediate subordinate to communicate the plan verbally to the bottom of the organizational layer, get their feedback, make additional modifications, and get further bottom-layer feedback before reporting results.

This pattern of communication can be more readily understood if the student will visualize the capital letter W. The original message goes down the left side of the W, hits bottom, comes back almost to the top in the center, goes down again, and finally emerges at the top right. The obstructive values of this Rebound, or Bouncing-Ball Gambit, are almost beyond description.

To fully appreciate the results that can be obtained from even the most basic approach to Expeditious Filteration, the student has only to look at the textbook application of Direct Expeditious Filteration employed by Clyde Wrecksales, General Manager of the Dilly Bolt Company. Clyde's job as General Manager was becoming altogether too boring. Bolts were being sold at an alarming rate, and no customer complaints had crossed Clyde's desk in almost three months. In fact, nothing had crossed his desk, and Clyde was beginning to worry about his retirement opportunities with the Dilly Bolt Company. It was then that he decided to employ the technique of Direct Expeditious Filteration to solve his own non-job problem.

Looking down his existing hierarchy, Clyde found to his dismay that there were only three levels between his exalted position and the front-line salesmen. Thus, his first move was an organizational one. He created the position of Assistant Sales Manager, which would now provide him with four levels between himself and the salesmen.

Reporting directly to Clyde was, of course, the Sales Manager, the new Assistant Sales Manager (who reported to the Sales Manager), and the salesmen (who reported now to the Assistant Sales Manager). Due to the extreme urgency brought on by increasing sales and profits and decreasing job responsibility, and recognizing that only four levels might not give the desired results, Clyde decided to risk implementation of Expeditious Filteration.

Clyde had noted that the most successful salesmen, and the ones who managed to retain customers over a number of years, spent a great deal of time and effort not only entertaining their customers, but also driving them in company cars to visit successful bolt installations. Thus, the objective now before him was to somehow dissolve this close customer/salesman relationship which had been built up over the years.

Recently, the company President had placed great emphasis on Dilly Bolt's effort in protecting the ecology. This gave Clyde the idea he needed to implement his obstructive strategy. He called in the Sales Manager and very carefully instructed him verbally on a new policy that Clyde wanted to have implemented and communicated verbally by the Sales Manager to the sales force as soon as possible. The policy was, "All salesmen will carry a can of disinfectant spray in their cars to help protect the ecology and their passengers."

After communicating these instructions to his Sales Manager, Clyde sat back and waited for the inevitable results of this seemingly simple communiqué.

He did not have long to wait. Within one week, the first cancellation came in from a customer who had been doing business with Dilly Bolt during the past twenty-five years. This was followed rapidly by other cancellations, irate letters and phone calls from both customers and prospects claiming that they had never been so insulted in their lives and never would do business with Dilly Bolt again.

Clyde was ecstatic. His system had worked perfectly, and all of a sudden he had a new job to do, rushing out to the field to correct these grave misunderstandings between the sales force and their treasured customers.

Since Clyde was an extremely conscientious obstructive manager, he took the time to investigate how his directive was relayed through each layer of his hierarchy, and fortunately preserved the evidence for posterity. Here is an exact transcript of how Clyde's message was communicated between each layer:

1.  *Clyde's original message to the Sales Manager:* "All salesmen will carry a can of disinfectant spray in their cars to help protect the ecology and their passengers."

2. *Sales Manager to Assistant Sales Manager:* "All salesmen will help ecology by carrying cars full of disinfectant spray for their passengers."

3. *Assistant Sales Manager to salesmen:* "You can help ecology by disinfecting your cars with spray, and passengers should be encouraged to use it."

4. *Salesmen:* "Before you let a customer in your car, spray him with disinfectant."

Thus, if the proper organization is in place, or if you can create it or use someone else's, there is no end to the devastation that can be caused through the effective use of Expeditious Filteration.

# 11: SYNERGISTIC REGRESSION

UP TO THIS POINT IN the text, each discussion of a technique has been directed toward the individual obstructive manager. This chapter explores an Obstructive Organizational Technique which can be applied by two or more obstructive managers working together for the utter destruction of an enterprise.

The *American Heritage Dictionary of the English Language* defines synergism as, "the action of two or more substances, organs, or organisms to achieve an effect of which each is individually incapable." Thus, Synergistic Regression means, "the action of two or more obstructive managers to achieve a regressive effect of which each is individually incapable."

Because of the need for two or more obstructive managers to accomplish Synergistic Regression, one of the first tasks confronting the obstructionist is to find others with whom he can identify. Actually, finding other obstructive managers with whom to work toward attainment of Synergistic Regression should not present too great a problem. Since it is the first step in the application of this principle, however, a quick survey of some of the most frequently-used approaches seems appropriate.

First, if you are building a new organization or have become part of an existing organization, consider hiring relatives. Relatives—particularly in-laws or distant cousins—seem to have a unique degree of aptitude for Obstructive Management. Many large, seemingly successful corporations have managed to constrict their profits and growth due to the synergistic effect of relatives on the payroll.

Second, if for some reason relatives are not available or legislated against, friends and former associates present the next most logical source of fellow obstructionists. This approach is most often used when an obstructive manager leaves his present company for a higher-level job with a new company. Friends and former associates rush to join him and quickly take up positions in the new firm to help him establish Synergistic Regression.

A third approach toward identification of other obstructive managers is to search diligently throughout the organization for individual obstructionists. Generally, they can be identified by their performance at staff meetings, through analysis of the output of their departments, or by charting the turnover

110

rate of their subordinates. Once banded together, these individual obstructionists can accomplish a high degree of Synergistic Regression.

A fourth and somewhat more time-consuming approach is to develop your own obstructionists from the ranks of seemingly competent management. This course of action is totally feasible according to Harrison's Law, which states, "within each of us there lurks a small seed of incompetence, which, if properly nurtured, can blossom forth into full-blooming obstructionism."

Once one or more obstructionists have been identified, it becomes necessary to organize them to achieve full Synergistic Regression. Here there exist two schools of thought concerning the most effective organizational structure. One school holds to the traditional direct-line approach of obstructionists reporting directly to each other. However, strong support is currently being shown for the informal, covert approach where obstructionists hold positions in nonrelated functions, but act together to block efficiency. This latter unstructured approach has proven highly successful in governmental bodies such as the Congress of the United States where obstructionists voting together can block any attempt at enlightened legislation.

The choice of establishing a direct or covert organization will, in the final analysis, be left up to the obstructionist. Such factors as his position in the organization, ultimate obstructive objectives, degree of threatened efficiency, and his own capabilities will help shape his decision as to the best approach to take.

To help the student fully understand the opportunities and potentials of Synergistic Regression, let's review the case of Stanley Starcross.

Over the past twenty years, Stanley Starcross had tried his best as an individual contributor to halt the progress of Yetch Systems, Inc. Despite his best obstructive efforts, Stanley had succeeded only in establishing the reputation of a "deep thinker" and "cautious evaluator." This, no doubt, was due to his reluctant participation in staff meetings and his tendency when faced with a decision to say, "Let me think it over and get back to you." The fact that he never got back to anyone had little bearing on the case.

Because of his established reputation, Stanley was appointed Director of Planning for Yetch Systems, Inc., and was charged with the responsibility of planning for future growth.

In his new position, Stanley was appalled by the progressive plans being submitted for his review by diligent line and staff managers. Many of the plans, if allowed to be carried to fruition, threatened the very existence of several management layers and promised a totally unacceptable rate of growth.

Stanley realized that despite his own expert obstructive expertise, he could not stem the tide of progress. The only answer was the immediate application of Synergistic Regression!

Since time was running out, Stanley could not

wait to staff other parts of the organization with relatives or friends. Also, his position did not permit a direct-line approach. His only choice was to attempt to establish quickly a covert organization to carry out Synergistic Regression.

Looking around the organization for clues toward identifying latent obstructionist talents, Stanley recalled that at a recent staff meeting the Manpower Development Manager, Peter Placement, had launched into a tedious but highly impassioned defense of a ponderous management-by-objectives approach being used by another company. Further investigation revealed that this same manager was secretly developing an extremely complex system of career pathing which involved numerous progression steps within each area of specialization, and ultimately would be controlled by a computer program. He indeed was a very promising potential for obstructive development.

In another functional area, Stanley observed with delight the growing personnel turnover rate being experienced in the Production Department. Sure enough, upon closer scrutiny, Stanley uncovered another ally in the presence of Maxwell Makem, the Production Manager, whose policies on working relationships were causing the turnover. Stanley was now ready to employ Synergistic Regression.

It was just in time, too, because at the next day's staff meeting, an efficient Personnel Manager submitted a long-range plan calling for a totally new approach toward hiring high-potential managers.

The aim of this plan was to consciously recruit top graduate-school students who would eventually take over key jobs at Yetch Systems, Inc.

The President quickly approved the concept, and it would have been unanimously agreed upon had not Stanley, recognizing the danger, said, "It sounds like a terrific idea—let me think it over and in a few days get back to you with some details on how it can become part of our company-wide program."

This clever stall gave Stanley the opportunity to consult with his covert organization, consisting of Peter Placement and Maxwell Makem. The three of them held a meeting in Stanley's garage and developed the following plan:

1. Stanley would have his department get to work immediately developing a probabilistic forecast on the results of the new personnel approach plus generating a list of strategy alternates. These alternates would include such options as buying known (obstructive) talent from competitive companies, giving advancement opportunities to existing (unqualified) workers, plus several others.

2. Peter Placement agreed to design a multi-step career path for the high-potential graduate students which would give them a "solid background in every facet of Yetch Systems operations."

3. Maxwell Makem agreed to study his own department and identify long-term training slots which could be used as starting points for the new graduate students.

Stanley presented his probabilistic forecast showing the probability of success for the graduate students and a list of strategy alternatives. The members present at the staff meeting were enthusiastic, particularly since Stanley endorsed the Personnel Manager's plan even though cautioning that if it did not work, the company could switch to one of his alternates.

The Manpower Development Manager, Peter Placement, heartily endorsed the Personnel Manager's plan and presented an elaborate chart depicting the multi-step career path he had developed for the graduate students.

The Production Manager, Maxwell Makem, proudly announced that he had identified ten entry-level positions within his department, which would give the students an immediate feel for the importance of production at Yetch Systems.

Synergistic Regression had taken effect. Working together, Stanley and his covert team had managed to totally nullify a threat of efficiency.

Even though the graduate students were hired, only three out of ten managed to survive the demeaning work in the Production Department. The three who remained have since left the company after being shunted from department to department without the chance of doing any real work as part of the "career development plan."

Stanley's strategic alternative of buying known talent has now been accepted—which will provide further expansion and greater opportunities for Synergistic Regression.

Thus, in summary, if you find yourself in a position where your own efforts are not enough to halt the tide of progress, employ Synergistic Regression to achieve together what could not be done alone.

# 12: SYNCHRONIZED DISCONTINUITY

DOCTOR QUANTI FYA-
ble, Dean of the Marketing Department at Learn Less University, was in a quandary. The recent graduates from his department had all secured jobs with leading marketing organizations and reportedly were doing extremely well.

Reviewing the objectives of his department— which were, "to make relevant courses of study available to students which will qualify and prepare them for specific careers in marketing"—Dean Fyable recognized he had a real problem. He was meeting all of the needs associated with his objective and was on the very verge of over-efficiency.

This revelation caused an exhaustive search for the cause of the threatened efficiency. The results of this search produced the following facts:

1. Students bent on pursuing marketing careers were being allowed to take relevant courses at the right time and with no difficulty in enrollment.
2. Communications training, which is a vital part of the marketing curriculum, was being taught as a practical workshop where students were encouraged to practice and critique each other on all forms of marketing communications.
3. Quantitative decision making was being taught as it pertains to making real marketing decisions, not just as a mathematical discipline.
4. Businessmen, without the required academic degrees, were being used as Adjunct Professors to bring real-world experience into the classroom.

Dean Fyable had isolated the real causes of efficiency. Now it was up to him to take the necessary corrective measures. The obvious answer was the immediate application of Synchronized Discontinuity. He had to figure out some way to retain the impact in each area while at the same time disrupting the synchronization which was producing efficiency.

His first move was relatively easy to accomplish. With a quick call to the Admissions Office, Dean Fyable was able to change the catalog course offering to make it virtually impossible for a student to attend the required courses during a normal four-year program.

Next, he zeroed in on communications training. Since communication involves the use of the five senses—hearing, seeing, smelling, touching, and tasting—Dean Fyable reasoned that the communications training course logically should be taught by the one faculty member most knowledgeable about parts of the human anatomy.

Following up on this thought, he contacted the Pre-Med School and quickly interested the Eye, Ear, Nose, and Throat specialist in taking over the communication program. The EENT specialist jumped for joy at the thought of teaching potential marketers the real value of anatomy.

Solving the quantitative decision-making problem was also easier than Fyable had expected. It took very little persuading to convince the head of the Math Department that a quantitative methods theory course should be a prerequisite to decision making. Of course, the theory course would be taught by a leading professor whose published works are still baffling the greatest minds in the country.

Dean Fyable's final move was to legislate that any businessman acting as an Adjunct Professor must possess a Ph.D. in Education, and further, that such businessmen could be used only during a summer semester. This latter requirement was supposed to encourage businessmen to take their vacations teaching at Learn Less University. In practice, it meant

119

that the students would be on vacation, so no real exposure to the business world could take place. With these four comparatively easy actions, Dean Fyable had effectively employed Synchronized Discontinuity to halt the growth of efficiency.

The student should note that in each case Dean Fyable did not necessarily lower the quality of the courses being offered. In fact, from a purely academic standpoint, quality was actually increased. Any student now graduating with a degree in marketing had a complete understanding of anatomy, advanced mathematical models, and business education. Naturally, very few graduate, and those who do generally evolve back into higher education.

From Dean Fyable's standpoint, Synchronized Discontinuity has been a great success. His paper on "Marketing Curriculum Development, a Didactic Approach," won honors at a recent association meeting. His stellar coordination with the Pre-Med School, the Math Department, and Admissions earned him much credit, and it is rumored that he is being considered for further promotion to Provost.

Greater elaboration is necessary before the obstructive student should attempt to implement this strategy. It can be used in all types of organizations as a hedge against efficiency. It is particularly useful in business organizations where the so-called Marketing Concept is practiced.

A noted author and educator once defined the effective implementation of the Marketing Concept as "the orchestration of effort." He then went on to describe how all elements in the company should work together toward the satisfaction of the customers' wants and needs.

Some companies have actually achieved such orchestration of effort through proper organization, staffing, and coordination. However, as any student of Obstructive Management can plainly see, this can quickly lead to over-efficiency. Thus, in recent years, excellent obstructive work has been done which has largely nullified attempts at orchestration of effort. In fact, the orchestra has become a rock group with everyone doing his own thing.

The concept of Synchronized Discontinuity is the organization approach most often applied by obstructive managers when faced with a smoothly running, well-coordinated effort.

Before attempting to apply Synchronized Discontinuity, it is necessary to carefully identify the prime objective of the organization. For example, in the Learn Less University case just described, the real objective was "to make relevant courses of study available to students which will qualify and prepare them for specific careers." A town government might have as its objective "to manage and provide those services necessary for the well-being and growth of the residents." A company's objective could be "to provide those goods and services which will best satisfy the customers' wants and needs."

The reason it is necessary to identify the prime objective is that by so doing, the obstructive manager can isolate those departments whose harmony of effort is essential. Once identified, an organizational structure can be devised which will prevent or at least inhibit coordination.

The critical thrust of Synchronized Discontinuity is toward disrupting continuity of effort. Now it is relatively easy to create a structure which totally prevents optimum performance. However, the subtlety of Synchronized Discontinuity requires maximum performance from each component, but peaking at a time that is out of synchronization with other components.

In attempting to apply Synchronized Discontinuity, the student should establish some definite goals or objectives which can be reached within any given organization. Some such goals might be the blocking of coordinating efforts, the realignment of reporting relationships, and the segmentation of presently cohesive functions.

One General Manager in a major corporation managed to split his Marketing Department into two separate groups. One group was headed by the Marketing Manager, who controlled product developing, pricing and advertising, and promotion. The other group was headed by the Sales Manager, who supposedly was responsible for the sale of all the products. By blocking communications between these two groups, Synchronized Discontinuity was accomplished. The marketing group now develops products, prices, and promotions which the sales group knows nothing about and feels are inappropriate for the marketplace.

This is but one example of the many ways this Obstructive Technique can be applied. Actually, applicable situations for Synchronized Discontinuity can be found everywhere. The only limitations are the innate abilities of the obstructive managers who must implement the concept. It is hoped that this chapter has equipped you for the challenge ahead.

# III

## CONTROLLING

# 13: FREE-FLOWING CENSORSHIP

IF THE OBSTRUCTIVE manager is not in complete control at all times, he can be engulfed by efficiency. For this reason, obstructionists down through the years have developed a series of controlling techniques that should be applied continuously to keep efficiency in check.

One of the greatest threats to inefficiency is a free-flowing internal communications system. If no rumors manage to run rampant, the workers will all understand what management is attempting to do. Individuals will be able to exchange ideas freely, problems will diminish, and productivity is bound to increase. And with the falloff of problems, of course, comes the reduced need for management.

In response to this very real need, obstructive managers employ the strategy of Free-Flowing Censorship—a technique whereby the manager proclaims the desire for a free flow of information, while at the same time methodically censoring all communications.

Free-Flowing Censorship should be used continuously, and its application must be well understood by all obstructionists.

One of the greatest masters of this controlling technique is Colonel Beauford Little, U.S.A. Retired. Just recently, he had another opportunity to demonstrate the power of Free-Flowing Censorship.

Through a series of proxie battles a new, enlightened management had seized control of Do Nothing Associates, and Colonel B. Little, Director of Strategic Planning, was in a quandary.

Rumors had been flying all through the organization concerning contemplated changes. Quite naturally, the employees were concerned and productive time was being lost discussing the latest "word" with associates.

To be responsive to this situation, the new top management suggested that each department manager call a meeting of his whole department, including all of the secretaries. At this meeting, the manager was to encourage his workers to cite all of the rumors they had heard in a sort of brainstorming session. Once all of the rumors were listed on a chalk board, the manager was to review them, showing why each was unfounded, and promise his department he would see to it that they received accurate information from him. Further, the manager was to encourage his department to meet with him individually or collectively any time they became concerned about something they had heard. These meetings would be properly followed up and the facts brought back to subordinates concerning the present situation.

The disastrous implications of this type of action are rather obvious. By showing such concern, the manager would increase the degree of trust and respect the employees have for him, and the overall results of this increased stature would, inevitably, be improved efficiency.

Colonel B. Little's response to this threat was typical for a great obstructionist. Recognizing the need to counterbalance the new top management's logical approach, he quickly employed a variation of Free-Flowing Censorship called the Trust Me Gambit.

He called a meeting of all of his department, including the secretaries. The meeting was held in the hallway in front of his office which forced everyone to remain standing throughout the proceedings. The Colonel opened by saying, "This won't take long because I want you all back at work. I have heard that people from my department are discussing rumors about the pending reorganization. Now I want you to trust me—if there is anything important for you to know I will tell you. I can't have you wondering about all the company, so from now on I don't want to hear of any of you spreading rumors. Trust me. The meeting is over."

Because of this prompt action, inefficiency increased as did distrust and future dissatisfaction. All of this created new problems for him to act upon and thereby helped to preserve his job.

Barely a week had passed when the same enlightened top management group recognized that, from time to time, workers within a department come into contact with high-level executives. They felt this could be a chance for a top executive who was interested in an element of the work being performed to talk directly to a worker, show interest, and to feed back the news of the meeting to the worker's department manager.

Top management suggested that department managers discuss this subject with all of their people, encourage them to introduce themselves to executives, and freely discuss any work element the executive showed interest in. Also, the managers were to offer to reinforce and back up whatever their subordinates said. This would help create a pride in the work which was being accomplished.

Colonel B. Little was aghast at the thought of a free-flowing exchange between his workers and top management. With such contact, top management might learn who was really doing the work. Some of his better workers might even get promoted, and his credibility could be severely damaged.

As a countermeasure, the good Colonel decided to attack with still another Free-Flowing Censorship tactic known in the vernacular as the "Gag Them Gracefully Ploy." After calling a meeting of all his people, he opened by saying, "It has come to my attention that some of you have held conversations with top executives in elevators and even in their offices. Now we do not want top management getting any incorrect view of what our department is doing. So if by some chance a top executive stops you in the hall, I want you to tell me right away. This way, I can be prepared to correct any misunderstandings. I have your best interests at heart and I am the only one who really understands the big picture."

As a result of this meeting, the workers now speak to no one. Most of all, they avoid top executives. The Colonel is able to control what top management hears about his department—which is usually that he is the one who thinks of each new idea.

Two weeks later, Colonel B. Little was forced to stave off still another challenge. A memo came floating down from the top stating that department managers were encouraged to allow subordinates to author and sign all reports and correspondence. This would permit other managers to review and recognize the ability of the individual workers. Department managers were to become involved in the preparation of reports only if they could make a real contribution. Department managers were to receive copies of only the major reports, not the routine information-gathering memoranda.

The Colonel knew from a past sad experience that allowing subordinates to originate and sign reports and memos would boost morale and allow top management to readily identify effective subordinates.

Seeing only the major reports would reduce drastically his already slim workload. The free flow of memos between departments would create intracompany cooperation which could lead to vastly improved efficiency.

Faced with this grave situation, the Colonel called in his secretary and dictated the following office memorandum:

```
To:        All Department Personnel
Subject:   Memo and Reporting Procedure

    Effective immediately, all memos and re-
ports originating in this department must
be signed by me. This is necessary to in-
crease the prestige of our operation, which
will benefit all of us. To facilitate this,
section managers will submit drafts of pro-
posed memos and reports to my office five
days prior to the intended release date.
Final  copies  containing  any  necessary
editing will then be prepared for my signa-
ture. This will ensure continuity of format
and consistency of high quality.

                    B. Little, Col. U.S.A. Ret.
```

This memo is still another variation of Free-Flowing Censorship. The intent is to censor everything but to make the subordinates freely agree to the process. It is sometimes called "The Writer's Cramp Crimp."

Naturally, as a result of this speedy action, top management felt Colonel B. Little was doing all of the work. This was further reinforced by his having to work late every night and on weekends editing reports and memos. Morale sank considerably lower, giving the Colonel numerous opportunities to counsel disgruntled employees and providing even greater justification for his job.

The final test of Colonel B. Little's adroitness in the application of Free-Flowing Censorship came about three weeks later.

From time to time, professional employees are invited by industry associates or civic groups to make public appearances. Such appearances provide an opportunity for individual recognition and serve to create a favorable public image for the company.

The new, enlightened corporate management encouraged this activity, feeling that the exposure of qualified professionals benefited both the company and the individual employee.

The Colonel saw immediately that the virtually unrestrained public appearances of professionals could lead to their being hired by other companies. Any such recognition would make them more promotable and more dissatisfied with their present status and pay scale. Also, the Colonel himself would appear unimportant if his professionals were invited to speak instead of him.

Recognizing the inherent dangers if this situation went unchecked, he promptly issued the following directive to professionals within his department:

To:        All Professional Employees
Subject:   Public Speaking Engagements

It has been noted that from time to time some of you are asked to fill speaking engagements for outside organizations.

To facilitate the efficient conduct of such appearances and insure that the most qualified individual makes the requested presentations, the following procedures will be immediately implemented:

1. All requests for outside appearances will be directed to my office.
2. I will assign the most qualified individual to prepare a script complete with appropriate visualization.
3. When and if, in my estimation, the situation warrants it, I will be available to make the actual presentation, thereby lending whatever prestige my position may hold to the occasion.

                    B. Little, Col. U.S.A. Ret.


Here students should particularly notice the implied compliance with top management's directive. This approach to Free-Flowing Censorship employs the "sweet-and-sour" strategy of raising expectations while actually censoring speech.

Quite naturally, top management feels that Colonel B. Little is truly the most knowledgeable and sought-after individual in the company. He is apparently qualified to speak on a wide range of technical subjects that require an unusual amount of professional expertise. He has received several offers from outside companies which he now is carefully considering.

In summary, the potential obstructive manager should employ the controlling technique of Free-Flowing Censorship whenever a communications situation develops which could in any way threaten his status quo. The primary obstructive objective is to control all written and verbal communications, thus creating an impression of an all-knowing and all-important manager.

# 14: AFFIRMATIVE ABANDONMENT

DOWN THROUGH THE years, management texts have preached religiously the dogma of incisive decision making. At all levels, managers are looked to as arbitrators and leaders who resolve conflicts and render decisions. Too much of this can lead only to efficiency and thereby threaten the existing state of affairs.

Obstructive managers, needing a technique to combat this dangerous situation, have developed the concept of Affirmative Abandonment. Simply put, the strategy requires that the manager affirm his absolute leadership position, and then totally abandon the function he is supposed to lead.

This abandonment produces a dramatic effect upon subordinates. Reactions have been known to range from total submissiveness to outright aggression. The most common reaction of all seems to be a form of progressive paranoia.

When properly applied, Affirmative Abandonment supplies the manager with several distinct advantages. First, it frees him from all work connected with the function he is supposed to manage. This freedom gives him an unlimited opportunity to engage full time in high-level company politics. This will eventually get him promoted to a far more attractive position where he can practice other Obstructive Techniques.

Second, the department that he has abandoned, striving to cope without a leader, will never increase its output or efficiency. True, some of the sharper subordinates may function effectively in a leaderless environment, but in the main, the work produced will be less than spectacular. Thus, the threat of over-efficiency can be successfully neutralized.

Application of this principle requires a certain degree of finesse. The key to this lies in the manner in which the obstructive manager affirms his leadership position.

A group can and will function quite well without a manager, so the mere absence of a manager is not the factor which causes the paranoia and other violent reactions. The frustration, disillusionment, and anger are brought on by the group's recognition that they have a leader who supposedly is there to care for them but who apparently has abandoned them in their time of need.

To help the student fully understand and appreciate the effectiveness of Affirmative Abandonment, the author learned of a famous practitioner of this obstructive principle and actually planted an agent to do undercover research while working in this manager's department. The following notes were smuggled out at great personal risk to both the author and the agent.

January 1    Got the job. I will be working in the Market Research Department as a Senior Researcher. It was just announced that Subject Manager will be taking over this department on January 3.

January 20    Subject Manager arrived today. He has a very likable personality, is a sharp dresser, and has the reputation of being a real "comer" in this corporation. After shaking hands with everyone, he announced a staff meeting set for January 25. He stated he would like to hold it sooner but that he had to meet the Marketing Vice-President in Nassau to travel with him on the company plane to Bermuda. All of the workers seemed pleased to feel their new boss is

139

so important. Morale is high in anticipation of the January 25 staff meeting.

January 25   Subject Manager phoned in this morning to tell his secretary that he could not hold today's scheduled staff meeting because he had to join the Executive Vice-President in San Francisco. Later, Subject Manager's secretary brought a note around to all the workers telling them that the meeting had been changed to January 30. Some workers grumbled a little since they had already changed their travel plans to be in on the twenty-fifth, but generally morale remains high.

January 30   Subject Manager's secretary delivered copies of a letter he had apparently dictated over the phone. The letter stated that he was very concerned about not being with us. As our manager, the letter went on, he knows how hard his absence must be on us. However, he has been asked to do a special report for the

President and won't be back for about a month. If anything of critical importance comes up, we are supposed to send him a letter through his secretary. Morale is slipping. One researcher is busy bringing his resumé up to date. Another is rushing around saying, "How am I supposed to get my work completed? I need a decision from our manager."

February 29    Another note delivered by Subject Manager's secretary. Apparently, she has appointed herself Manager-in-Absentia. The note says that Subject Manager has heard that some of us are not reporting to work on time in the morning and that he has asked his secretary to check on us. The signature looks a little funny, so I am not really sure who wrote the note. Morale is sinking rapidly. Several major projects have been stopped entirely. Three researchers are actively seeking new jobs. Several others have seemingly drawn themselves into a shell and don't speak to anyone any more. One researcher is getting progressively more paranoid every day. He now goes from office to office saying such things as, "Why doesn't he like me? What are we doing here? Do you suppose he has been told to treat us this way? Do you suppose the entire company has forgotten us?"

March 30    A rumor was started that someone had seen Subject Manager over the weekend at the office. However, there was no physical evidence to support it except that his secretary has suddenly ordered all new furniture for his office. The tension increases daily. I don't know how much longer I will be able to take it. One researcher, needing a decision, attempted to go over Subject Manager's head and promptly got turned down with the admonition to go through Subject Manager. No new projects have been started in the last month. Saw a picture of Subject Manager in the company newspaper. He was boarding the company jet with the President on the way to San Juan for a management meeting.

April 30    A letter from Subject Manager was delivered today by his secretary just before we read about his promotion in the company paper. The letter said that he had enjoyed working with us, and while he recognized that he did not spend as much time as he would have liked to with us, he knew we all would understand. He further stated that he had personally handpicked a manager to replace him who would be able to provide a continuation of the policies that he had established. I QUIT.

In summary, the subtle techniques employed in the application of Affirmative Abandonment can be adapted to fit almost any type of organization. At the time the obstructive manager takes over, the initial good impression is of critical importance. This raises the expectations of the workers and really sets them up for total abandonment.

Using a secretary as a go-between is a masterful

approach. It further separates the obstructionist from his workers, and frequently leads to false interpretations of his written messages. In such situations, it is quite common for the secretary to assume a leadership role on her own which will cause even further confusion and generally infuriate the workers.

By abandoning the management function, the obstructionist is perfectly free to pursue company politics with the full expectation of being promoted to a high-level position. Work in the abandoned department will diminish, and invariably one or two of the better workers will quit. This provides a great opportunity for whoever replaces this particular obstructionist to do some creative hiring and even some application of the Obstructive Planning and Organizing Techniques which have been discussed earlier in this text. Thus, all in all, the concept of Affirmative Abandonment is a highly workable controlling technique which almost certainly can paralyze and stifle the creativity within any organization.

# 15: MAGNANIMOUS AUTOCRACY

ONLY RECENTLY WAS
the concept of Magnanimous Autocracy identified
and classified as an Obstructive Technique. In earlier times, a manager who followed the principles of
this concept was looked upon as a truly productive
leader, a company man, and a real "go-getter." But
new investigations have proven that the results obtained through the applications of this controlling
technique fall definitely within the perimeters of the
practice of obstructive management.

To uncover the true nature of this technique, a
team of investigators for the specially convened Senate Committee Investigating Unclassified Obstructive Management Techniques spent many months
gathering data. The approach used by the investigators was to study the attitudes of workers who
reported to a manager controlling via a method
which was suspected of being an Obstructive Technique. Not only were the attitudes of the workers

examined, but also the attitudes of top management within the same company. It was found that the workers' views contrasted sharply with those of top management, particularly in response to the question, "How do you view the leadership qualities being employed by this manager?"

To a man, top management responded in every case with such accolades as: superior, true team champion, dynamic, considerate, and excellent!

The responses from workers, however, followed the line of: pompous ass, self-centered, dictatorial, inconsiderate, and magnanimous S.O.B.

This dichotomy of views caused the investigators to probe more deeply and eventually discover the true obstructive principles of Magnanimous Autocracy.

Since this new technique shows tremendous promise, the manager who was first discovered to be employing it was called to make a special appearance before the Senate Committee Investigating Unclassified Obstructive Management Techniques. The following is a brief transcript of the major part of the hearing. The Chairman of this Committee was Senator Ham Nervin, Democrat from Louisiana.

| | |
|---|---|
| SEN. NERVIN: | Boy, y'all's in big trouble. You been practicin' an Obstructive Technique which has not been duly authorized by this here committee— |
| MANAGER: | I don't see how you can call it obstructive. I have done very |

well for myself, and my company President thinks I am just great!

SEN. NERVIN: Ah don' care 'bout your President, ah do care 'bout your workers, the pore folk who have to work fo' you. They feel you all's an obstructionist!

MANAGER: They do alright. I see they get their raises on time, have good working conditions, and get all the other benefits. I can't help it if some of them quit. I think they are just plain lazy!

SEN. NERVIN: Let's not be callin' those boys lazy! Let's look at the record. It says here that on June 10 at a staff meetin' you volunteered yourself to be Chairman of the Blood Drive for your company. Is that right?

MANAGER: Yes, sir.

SEN. NERVIN: It also says that the results of the Blood Drive was the most successful one they ever held. Is that right?

MANAGER: Yes, sir. I am very, very proud of my accomplishment.

SEN. NERVIN: As a result of this, y'all were given the Blood Chairmanship of the Year Award?

MANAGER: Yes, sir. I have a bag of blood

framed and hanging in my office.

SEN. NERVIN:	Now ah'd like to read into the record a sworn statement from one of your workers. It says here that on June 11 y'all called a meetin' of those workers. Y'all told them that all vacations would be cancelled unless each donated a pint of blood and each got two workers from other departments to donate blood. What'd you say 'bout that?

MANAGER:	I was just trying to promote a little bit of team spirit. I told them that I needed their cooperation and that they'd better do it or else. They did it, and I won.

SEN. NERVIN:	This here statement goes on to say that the work in the department fell way behind durin' this period 'cause they were all rushin' around givin' blood or chasin' others to give blood.

MANAGER:	That's why I say they're lazy. I told them that their work had better not slip or I would fire them.

SEN. NERVIN:	But y'all were expectin' them to do extra work on this here

148

|  | blood campaign in addition to their regular work. Somethin' has to give. |
|---|---|
| MANAGER: | A little extra work never hurt anyone, and a little extra outside work won't hurt anyone either. It certainly made our department look very good and particularly helped me. |
| SEN. NERVIN: | Did y'all do any extra work? |
| MANAGER: | Of course not, I was the Chairman! |
| SEN. NERVIN: | Now let's consider some of your other actions. Durin' the past year, the record shows that y'all have been: Chairman of the United Fund Drive, Leader of a Study Team Investigating Company Participation in Civic Activities, Chairman of the Annual Golf Outing, Organizer of the Shareholders' Meeting, and Program Chairman of the Executive Vice President's Retirement Party—is this record correct? |
| MANAGER: | Yes, sir, except you left out a few of my other accomplishments in some of the civic organizations and technical societies to which I belong. |
| SEN. NERVIN: | Is it also true that in each of |

these activities your workers were ordered or coerced into doin' all the actual work plus tryin' to perform their regular jobs?

MANAGER: We've got to make our department look good. I don't like the word "coerced." I just told them to do it or I would fire them.

SEN. NERVIN: Ah think we all have heard enough. Y'all definitely an obstructive manager and are to be commended for developin' a new technique for lowerin' overall efficiency while increasin' your own stature. The magnanimous gestures y'all make in offerin' your services coupled with the autocratic approach toward controllin' your workers is an exemplary performance. By your actions, y'all have set a model of Magnanimous Autocracy to be followed by future practitioners of Obstructive Management down through the years. This hearin' is adjourned.

# 16: DYNAMIC LETHARGY

ALWAYS RIGHT SYStems, Incorporated, has always enjoyed a leadership position in its field. Its stock is traded at a fast pace and is always profitable. Its products are always better than those of its competitors and its workers always busy.

Controlling the growth and profitability of this dynamic company has always been the job of the Right family. Reginald Right, the current President and Chief Executive Officer, is the son of the Board Chairman, Rufus Right. Other Rights are scattered throughout the organization to ensure that the right decisions are made at the right time. All in all, Always Right Systems, Inc., presents a perfect image of the right way to run an organization.

This atmosphere of super-efficiency is not due to the efforts of any one of the members of the Right

151

family. It is directly traceable to one obstructive department manager who has mastered the controlling technique of Dynamic Lethargy. Neither Reginald nor Rufus Right will admit it in public, but both know that without the Analysis and Development Department headed by a distant cousin, Percy Circle, Always Right Systems, Inc., could never have achieved its spectacular success.

Percy Circle joined Always Right Systems thirty-two years ago when Rufus Right's wife insisted he do something for her cousin to snap him out of his lethargy. When faced with dire alternatives, Rufus had agreed, and created the Analysis and Development Department, placing Percy at its head.

The original concept in establishing this department was to provide a multidiscipline group that could analyze and develop plans, ideas, and products which would later be turned over to operating departments for action.

During Rufus' regime, the Analysis and Development Department functioned with somewhat questionable results. It was staffed with highly competent engineers, systems analysts, behavioral scientists, and a smattering of marketing generalists. The work flowed through the department as shown in Figure 4, opposite.

Some good work came out of the department and was duly turned over to the operating departments for implementation. However, during Rufus' last years as President, he noticed that projects assigned to the Analysis and Development Department were taking increasingly longer times to emerge in usable

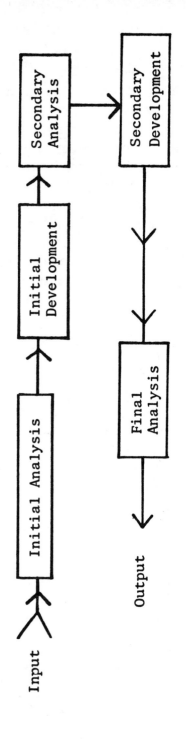

Figure 4:

ANALYSIS AND DEVELOPMENT DEPARTMENT
ORIGINAL WORK FLOW DIAGRAM

form. He attributed this partly to Percy's naturally lethargic personality and partly to the concern of the workers, who wanted to be sure they were right before turning over a project to operations. They all seemed to be extremely busy and a truly dynamic environment existed in the whole department.

Just prior to turning over the reins to his son Reginald, Rufus had fallen into the habit of assigning Percy only projects that were of lesser importance or ones where prolonged study could not affect the operation of the company.

Once or twice, when questioned by a shareholder, Rufus had found it quite handy to say that such and such was under active study in the Analysis and Development Department, knowing full well that he might never see the results of the study.

When Reginald Right ascended to the presidency, he and his father held many lengthy discussions trying to decide what to do with cousin Percy and his department. Percy himself finally resolved the dilemma for them by suggesting a slight reorganization that would permit him to control his organization in a manner more in keeping with his lethargic disposition.

Reginald, demonstrating a rare degree of foresight, seized upon this suggestion and authorized the change. Much to Percy's delight, the proposed workflow diagram shown in Figure 5, opposite, was immediately implemented.

With this new work flow in place, Percy had nothing to do except introduce new projects into the

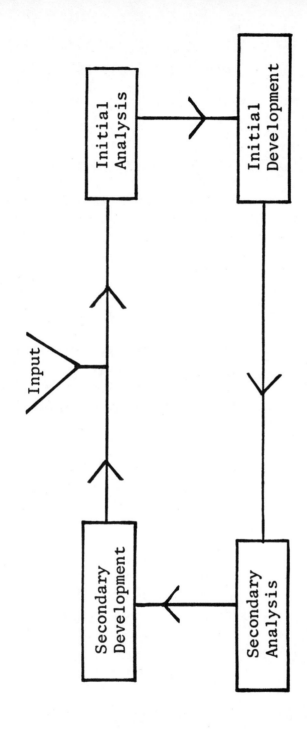

Figure 5:
ANALYSIS AND DEVELOPMENT DEPARTMENT
PROPOSED WORK FLOW DIAGRAM

system. He and his people no longer had to worry about being right and turning projects over to operations. Now they could study any idea indefinitely.

Reginald was also very happy. Through Percy's application of Dynamic Lethargy, he now had a department where everyone was busy producing nothing. Thereafter, whenever Reginald was plagued by government requirements such as Equal Opportunity and Minority Relations, Environmental Regulations, or Accident and Health Safety Regulations, he could turn the project over to the Analysis and Development Department, knowing full well that he would never see the results of the study and that any necessary action would be postponed indefinitely.

All inventors who presented unsolicited ideas to Always Right Systems, Inc., were also directed to Percy. Internally, Percy's department became the repository for the proposed pay plans, benefit packages, and a whole wide variety of organizational development schemes.

The existence of Percy's Analysis and Development Department freed the operating departments to quickly produce and market their own Right systems. This rapid response allowed them to beat out their competitors who were spending too much time themselves analyzing and developing new ideas.

All in all, it has been a most successful concept and is definitely responsible for the dynamic growth of Always Right Systems, Inc.

The principles which can be learned from this

case are valuable to the student of obstructive management. First of all, Dynamic Lethargy creates an environment in which the doing of the work is more important than the output of the function. Work is carried out at a dynamic, fast-moving pace, but due to the lethargy of the leader, no significant accomplishments are ever produced.

The department manager of such an operation is always sure of a job, since his department is vital to the survival of the parent company. Best of all, he has nothing important to do except to introduce new projects into the work-flow process within his department. This allows him to be almost totally lethargic.

The workers in the department are always busy referring projects onto the next step within the department. When a project comes around the second or third time, it has been changed so drastically that the workers feel it is a totally new assignment and attack it with never-ending zeal.

Top management can make effective use of such an operation to relieve them from taking unpopular actions. When questioned, they are able to say with total honesty, "It is being worked on in the Analysis and Development Department."

# 17: CONCENTRATED CONSTRICTIONISM

ONE OF THE MOST TRY-ing tasks for an obstructionist manager is the continuous control of creativity. Creativity, if allowed to run rampant within an organization, can quickly lead to over-efficiency, high morale, and a great reduction of problems for managers to solve.

In the chapter on Flexible Rigidity, it was demonstrated how an obstructive manager can control creativity, provided the organization has established hard-and-fast policies. However, creativity is apt to crop up any time in any organization. Thus, there is a need for a technique that can be applied quickly to control it. Concentrated Constrictionism meets this need as a fast-acting, autocratic answer to creeping creativity.

Fortunately for the students of Obstructive Management, the world's greatest authority on con-

159

straints, Professor Ludwig von Basham, consented
to an interview focused on the subject of instant
corrective action to be taken to halt the growth of
creativity.

Professor von Basham has acted as a consultant
on anti-creativity ever since his services were no
longer needed as a concentration camp commander
during World War II. He is usually called in by a
company when, through carelessly efficient management, creativity is totally out of control and the only
solution is a blitzkrieg.

The following interview was conducted by the
author at von Basham's home deep in the Black
Forest.

| | |
|---|---|
| AUTHOR: | Thank you, Professor von Basham, for granting this interview . . . |
| VON BASHAM: | Let's get on with it. I have a lot of work to do. Creativity is cropping up all over these days. |
| AUTHOR: | When a client calls you in to identify and eliminate creativity, what is the first thing you do? |
| VON BASHAM: | I wander around and look at offices and people. |
| AUTHOR: | Offices and people? What does that tell you? |
| VON BASHAM: | Dumkoff! If the offices are well-decorated, quiet, and pleasant |

to work in, and all the people seem happy, and enjoy talking to each other, creativity is bound to be lurking somewhere.

AUTHOR: In what department are you most likely to find creativity?

VON BASHAM: It can be found anywhere, of course, but a good place to look first of all is in the Advertising and Promotion Group. They usually think they are creative even if they aren't!

AUTHOR: How can you tell if they are really creative?

VON BASHAM: I read the advertising copy and check the promotion pieces looking for unusual or clever copy.

AUTHOR: Could you give us an example?

VON BASHAM: Yes. When I was working with the Rhine Maiden Wine Company, I noticed that some schweinhund had changed the label design from the traditional muscular woman, wearing armor and carrying a spear while guarding the grapes, to a sexy blond emerging from the Rhine River wearing a topless bikini and pushing two wine casks. The caption read—"Sip wine from my casks." That's creativity!

AUTHOR: What did you do?

VON BASHAM: I got that writer fired instantly and replaced him with a graduate engineer. There was no hope for him. He had already drafted another ad showing the same Rhine Maiden lying on top of a huge vat of wine, saying, "Savor me at bedtime."

AUTHOR: You are perfectly right. There was no hope for him. What are some other signs of creativity?

VON BASHAM: Blackboards in the offices.

AUTHOR: Blackboards?

VON BASHAM: Yah. This means that whoever works there can write ideas on the board, walk around the room, think, erase, change ideas, think more, and finally create!

AUTHOR: I never thought about it that way.

VON BASHAM: Yah. Thinking is dangerous. Blackboards should never be allowed, nor should flip charts or even large paper—only little paper pads. This forces people to think small if they must think at all.

AUTHOR: What other things help you spot creativity?

VON BASHAM: Wall plaques and bookcases.

AUTHOR: How do they help?

VON BASHAM: Wall plaques are usually presented for some accomplishment, in recognition of good work. Giving recognition for good work builds morale; it encourages people to think of new ideas. It must be stopped!

AUTHOR: Easy there, professor. What's wrong with bookcases?

VON BASHAM: Definitely bad, particularly in someone's office. Books are very dangerous. They contain ideas developed by authors who have had time to think. If an organization must have books, they should be locked up in one room and controlled by an illiterate librarian!

AUTHOR: Are there other signs that are characteristic of a creative environment?

VON BASHAM: Lighting, music, and carpets.

AUTHOR: How do they affect creativity?

VON BASHAM: Soft lighting, happy soft music, and deep, soft carpets are almost always indicators of creativity at work somewhere in the organization. They promote a relaxed, quiet environment that causes people to enjoy their work and think creative ideas.

AUTHOR: What do you do when you find this condition?

VON BASHAM: Tear up the carpets. Then the workers can hear the sound of marching feet in the halls. I play loud march music to keep them alert, and quickly install glaring fluorescent lighting everywhere so the whole place is as bright as day.

AUTHOR: All that sounds a bit extreme. Are there any other physical signs to watch for in an organization?

VON BASHAM: Yah. Couches and chairs.

AUTHOR: What's wrong with couches and chairs?

VON BASHAM: A couch is for relaxing or even sleeping. *There will be no sleeping on the job!* Extra chairs encourage other workers to visit and sit down. This leads to conversation and even group problem solving. Extra chairs must go!

AUTHOR: I guess with everybody standing up there isn't much chance for conversation. Earlier you mentioned Advertising and Promotion as dangerously creative departments. Are there any other dangerous departments you check into?

VON BASHAM: I check them all, particularly the Training and Education Department. Their personnel are usually the root of all the creative evil in any organization.

AUTHOR: How can the Training and Education Department affect creativity?

VON BASHAM: Affect it? They teach it! They run seminars on creative thinking, motivation, leadership styles, sensitivity, group experiences, and countless other workshops all designed to make managers more creative and efficient! Just getting managers together during a seminar is dangerous. They talk to each other and often come up with creative solutions! Training and Education is the most awesome threat to the status quo ever conceived. It must and will be stopped!

AUTHOR: You just can't go in and cut out all training.

VON BASHAM: Well, if I can't then at least I reduce it to on-the-job-training, limited to learning skills needed to operate equipment. A good autocratic manager does not need all that education. A good Corporal like the one I used to know, will *tell* the workers what to do. He can lead an entire country.

AUTHOR: Let's not get into old wartime stories. As a final question: What happens to an organization after you have stamped out creativity?

VON BASHAM: The status quo returns, work progresses at a dull, routine rate, the workers grumble and often quit, and many management jobs are created to help get the workers whipped back into line.

AUTHOR: Thank you, Professor von Basham. I know your comments will help future managers combat rising creativity.

VON BASHAM: It has been my pleasure. I hope the contribution I have made will help set the stage for a New Order in Management.

# 18: DRAMATIC NEGATIVISM

DURING THE BUSINESS career of every obstructive manager there comes a time when he becomes complacent, thinking he has enough problems to solve and he will surely be promoted. When this happens, the true obstructionist forces himself to re-evaluate his own actions with a view toward creating new frustrations within his group, and, if possible, demoralize the entire company.

The controlling technique used by past obstructionists when faced with complacency is Dramatic Negativism. This concept strikes directly at morale and invariably produces excellent negative results.

A simple definition of Dramatic Negativism is, "the act of being overly dramatic in the introduction of negative feelings." It is sometimes described in the vernacular as the "Oh, Christ, look what they've done to us now" syndrome. The objective of employing Dramatic Negativism is to create an atmosphere within a given department whereby the workers feel that all of management is against them. This sentiment tends to force the workers to rally around their Obstructive Manager in a futile battle against the system. If properly applied, a feeling of dissension often spreads to other departments, creating a minor mutiny.

In practice, Dramatic Negativism is quite easy to employ. All it takes is the will to destroy morale and the ability to convert into negative terms any and all actions, communications, and visits by top management.

Generally speaking, top management is quite willing to cooperate with an obstructive manager who wishes to introduce Dramatic Negativism. Hardly a day goes by in any organization when at least one member of the top management team does not take some action which, when properly dramatized, will have negative implications. It therefore falls to the obstructive manager to keep alert for these actions and provide the proper negative interpretation.

The simplicity of application and results to be obtained from this controlling technique can best be understood by the student through a review of the Sharp Screw Company case, which has become a classic for the study of Dramatic Negativism.

The Sharp Screw Company was founded in 1898 as a result of a government contract to supply screws for the Spanish American War. Since then, it has shown slow growth with minor expansion taking place as each new war developed.

After the Vietnam War, Sharp Screw Company went through a slight reorganization that placed three executives at its helm with a multitude of lesser Vice-Presidents reporting directly to this top group.

Norman Nurdquist had been Manager of Quality Control since the Korean War. Operating as a reasonably effective obstructive manager, he had been able to create enough problems to secure his job and was even being talked of as a candidate for a Vice-Presidency.

Norman was, however, a number two choice for the promotion, since the other candidate, the Manager of Engineering, had recently gained top management's favor by fouling up his section and then shifting the blame to one of his subordinates, who was subsequently fired.

Without fully realizing it, Norman had slipped into a state of complacency. Fortunately for him, he realized this during a recent staff meeting when all at once he had no real problems of any consequence to report and, subsequently, to solve.

Recognizing his now somewhat tenuous position, Norman decided immediately to employ Dramatic Negativism. The very next day, Norman attacked his in-basket with renewed vigor. Sure enough, buried between two expense accounts was a memo from top management restating the company policy on working hours.

Eagerly seizing the memo, Norman marched out

into his department and nearly shouted, "Have you all seen what they are doing to us?" Naturally no one had, since the memo had been hidden in Norman's in-basket. So all of the workers gathered around as Norman read with great disgust the company policy on working hours, adding at just the right times such comments as, "Boy, if we follow this, our jobs will be much tougher," and "These hours may be all right for top brass, but not for us working guys!"

The workers shouted their approval of Norman's comments and went back to work grumbling among themselves about the lack of understanding on the part of top management.

The next day, one of the top executives made a speech at a local businessmen's luncheon. The speech was reprinted in the local newspaper that Norman read the following morning. Grabbing a red marking pen, Norman quickly circled several comments which could effectively be misunderstood.

Later at the office, Norman went storming out again into the middle of his workers, waving the newspaper clipping and shouting, "Did you guys read this mess? Boy, it sure makes our department look bad. What are they doing to us?" Naturally, the workers had not read the clipping, so all stood around as Norman effectively misinterpreted several choice statements such as, "Quality control remains at the same high level," to which Norman added, "These guys don't realize how much we really improved." The statement, "Our rejection rate is below

Korean War levels" amplified by Norman became, "Those S.O.B.s don't know our rate is the best in the industry. They don't believe anything I tell them!"

Again, the workers grumbled. Some even shouted in defiance of top management and quickly sided with their boss, Norman.

The following day, one of the top management team decided to visit Norman on a matter of minor importance. Norman was ecstatic, since this gave him the opportunity to really apply Dramatic Negativism.

While the top manager was with Norman, Norman carefully kept his office door closed so his workers could not hear what was going on. Shortly after the Vice-President left, Norman slowly emerged from his office in an apparent state of total dejection. He ambled out among his workers shaking his head as if in disbelief. Naturally, the workers were concerned for their boss's well-being. They quickly clustered around him saying such solicitous things as, "What's the matter, boss?" "What did he do to you?" "Tell us what's wrong, boss." Norman spoke quietly, making an apparent valiant attempt to conceal burning anger. Through clenched teeth, Norman asked, "Do you guys know what that S.O.B. was doing?"

Naturally, the workers did not know since Norman's door had been closed the whole time. Almost in unison, the response was, "No, boss. Tell us! Tell us!" To which Norman slowly replied, "He was spying on us! Imagine, spying on us to see if we were

171

working. I tell you, no department is safe anymore. They're definitely out to get us all unless we get them first!" The workers clenched their fists and chanted, "Yeah, yeah, we'll help you, boss."

Sensing that the timing was right, Norman then carefully stated, "If I was a Vice-President, things would be different, but I guess I don't stand much of a chance since the top brass seems to be hipped on the Manager of Engineering. Boy, you know he won't ever understand our problems if he gets in!" The workers readily agreed and fairly snarled, "Don't worry, boss, we'll help you." And help they did, but in what way Norman may never know. The Manager of Engineering suddenly resigned, sold his house, and moved far away. Some who claim to have seen him say he is running a small gas station in the middle of the desert in Arizona.

Naturally, top management recognized Norman's obstructive tactics and talent, and quickly promoted him to Vice-President. It is rumored now that Norman's replacement—who once worked for Norman —has already made the statement to his workers, "What's that S.O.B. Norman trying to do to us?"

# 19: CONSCIENTIOUS INCOMPETENCE

THE ETERNAL QUEST for excellence in performance can in itself be a powerful obstructive controlling technique. Systems management spawns an uncontrollable urge to measure and quantify human performance. If carried to the proper extremes, this can produce dramatically negative results.

The concept of Conscientious Incompetence recognizes and responds to this obstructive need. Successful practitioners are invariably counted among the most conscientious managers in the world. Their infinite attention to detail, installation of elaborate measurement systems, and design of error-free reporting systems attests to their efforts to reach perfection.

There are two schools of obstructive thought concerning the requirements for Conscientious Incompetence. Both factions recognize the need for over-control as an important element. They disagree, however, sometimes violently, on the methods or approach to be used.

The form of Conscientious Incompetence which seems to attract the largest number of practitioners bases its strength upon the talents of the individual manager to nit-pick or exercise totally unnecessary controls over the work being generated within a department. His superiors usually describe this type of obstructionist as meticulous, painstaking, careful, and conscientious. In the day-to-day conduct of business within his department, he constantly reminds his subordinates that "Any work leaving this department reflects on all of us, so it *must* be perfect."

"Perfect" invariably means that the work must be in the boss's own words, done in his own style, and use his own format. Another characteristic of this school of Conscientious Incompetence is the heavy use of internal controls such as work-process planning forms, supply inventories, and other insidious control documents. Subordinates are never allowed to work on their own, nor are they permitted the luxury of making a mistake. The department members, working in such an environment, spend all of their time trying to guess exactly how the boss would say or write or execute a certain project. The result of this is a continual re-doing of projects, checking and rechecking every fact before submitting it for the obstructive manager's "approval."

The existence of such a manager benefits the company: His activities help insure the personnel manager's job due to the heavy turnover rate that can realistically be predicted. Top management can also use this department to slow down other more aggressive departments by putting the obstructive department manager in charge of a task force studying productivity. And the nit-picking department manager himself is almost assured of continued employment, since there is a great need within industry for meticulous, painstaking, careful, and conscientious leaders.

The other school of thought concerning Conscientious Incompetence holds that in order to practice this obstructive technique, the manager must have an impact upon a broad segment of his company. Within a hierarchy, he must hold a position of sufficient magnitude that his actions have direct impact upon the growth and profitability of the organization. Devotees of this form of Conscientious Incompetence view themselves as professionals and look upon the nit-picker almost as a trainee attempting to learn the true art of Conscientious Incompetence.

Trying to learn more about this style of obstructive management, the author contacted the Association for Association and Society Specialists, commonly known by its initials, AASS. A quick check of their membership revealed that there was indeed a society whose purpose is closely aligned with Conscientious Incompetence. It is called the Society for Inappropriate Controls and Knowledge, also commonly known by its initials, SICK.

SICK's Executive Secretary, when learning of the author's interest in Obstructive Management, quickly issued the author a verbal invitation to attend SICK's annual convention and witness the presentation of the prestigious Stifler of the Year Award. He assured me that the official formal invitation would be forthcoming, together with the necessary enrollment and historical data forms.

One month before the meeting, a special delivery, return receipt requested, large white envelope marked URGENT was delivered at 7:30 A.M. The envelope contained an engraved invitation marked R.S.V.P.; a five-page personal-history data questionnaire to be completed in triplicate and returned not later than three weeks prior to the meeting; and a three-page itinerary and mode-of-travel form to be returned in triplicate two weeks prior to the meeting. An itemized packing list to be checked off specifying how many pair of socks, shorts, ties, etc., I planned to bring along was to be filled out in its entirety—then one copy was to be left home, one copy was to be brought with me, and a third copy was to be mailed to Society Headquarters one week before the meeting.

Every few days until the start of the meeting, this initial mailing was followed by a variety of forms to be completed: instructions, meal menus, and a complete credit investigation.

Keeping ahead of this deluge of paperwork occupied every minute of each day. I almost missed the meeting completely because of a Self-interests, Objectives, and Results Measurement Form—apparently essential to the success of the entire meeting. My failure to complete this form properly was due to my inability to quantify the results that would accrue to me from a chamber music recital scheduled for Monday night. They finally accepted a results measurement based upon a computation of the time it takes for this form of entertainment to put me to sleep and use of this as a future measurement for tolerance of chamber music. I later discovered that the entire invitation and enrollment procedure is part of their membership requirement. Anyone who does not complete it properly and on time is automatically expelled from the society.

The highlight of the entire meeting was the Awards Banquet held on Wednesday evening. Attendance was limited to those who had successfully completed a three-page evaluation form critiquing each event, establishing measurement criteria, and accounting for each hour of participation time.

The award presented at this banquet is the famed Performance Stifler Plaque, given annually to the member who submits and has instituted the most complete array of reports, procedures, and control documents over the preceding year. Judging is done by the Stifling Committee, composed of twenty members who spend the entire year reading, evaluating, and reporting on the controlling procedures submitted annually by each member of the society. This is an extremely powerful committee, since it can reject a member's contribution for lack of complexity—which results in immediate expulsion.

The committee has developed an impressive evaluation procedure based on a computer program that synthesizes and tabulates data according to degree of complexity, frustration index, performance deficiency probabilities, and the relative unimportance of the data base. The results of this deliberation culminates in the annual selection of one obstructive member who has done the most to halt his organization's progress.

For a number of years, it seems, this award has been won by government workers, who apparently have a unique ability to identify and develop measurements for totally irrelevant activities. Last year's recipient owed his success largely to a sophisticated paperclip inventory procedure, a locked-desk report, and a complex blotter-destruction system.

With this long history of victorious civil servants, it was particularly gratifying when this year's winner turned out to be Dudley Dummer, General Sales Manager of Beastly Systems, Inc. The announcement of his name brought the participants to their feet for a standing ovation that lasted for three minutes and fifty-six seconds, a fact duly noted in the meeting minutes.

Dudley certainly deserved the Performance Stifler Plaque. In the short span of one year, he had instituted thirty-four reports which had forced the sales organization to replace all of its field managers and salesmen, thus creating numerous job opportunities for new personnel and reducing the sales volume to a trickle of accidental orders. This action permitted the executives of Beastly to write off the entire year as a loss against huge profits that had been previously accumulated.

The list of Dudley's reports was slowly read off to the assembled participants to the accompaniment of a muffled timpani drum roll supplied by the chamber music orchestra. Here is the complete list:

### Daily

    Time Utilization Reports
    Car, Toll, and Gasoline Reports
    Telephone Usage Reports
    Copy Machine Utilization Reports
    Stamp Usage Reports

### Weekly

    Expense Accounts
    Lost Order Reports
    Itinerary Planning Reports
    Prospect Activity Reports
    Auto Usage Reports
    Customer Complaint Report
    Inventory Control Report
    Accounts Receivable Report
    Time and Duty Analysis Report
    Telephone Expense Report

### Monthly

    Forecast of Unusual Sales
    Competitive Action Report

Analysis of Key Accounts
Sales Promotion Activities Report
Inventory Review
Key Work Objectives Review


## Quarterly

Review of Business Objectives
Review of Personal Objectives
Sales Forecast
Analysis of Strategic Plan


## Semiannual

Budget Forecast
Business Plan
Performance Review
Personal Development Plan


## Annual

Strategic Plan
Objectives and Opportunity Plan
Budget Versus Actual Review
Salary Review
Review of all Reviews


At the end of the reading, another standing ovation occurred for four minutes and twenty-four seconds during which time Dudley stood at attention with tears in his eyes. He was then presented with the Performance Stifler Plaque upon which was inscribed: "The Society for Inappropriate Controls and Knowledge proudly recognizes Dudley Dummer as the outstanding Performance Stifler of the Year. Your devotion to measuring time, performance, and costs, without regard to efficiency, is truly exemplary."

It was a very moving ceremony and a truly gratifying experience for the author. Students of obstructive management who apply themselves and institute the technique of Conscientious Incompetence may themselves one day be standing before this prestigious society to receive the Stifler of the Year Award.

# 20: CONSEQUENTIAL RETALIATION

IN THE PRACTICE OF Obstructive Management Techniques, it is highly important that top management be involved continuously with minor daily business problems. This keeps them from doing any long-range planning that could lead to improved effectiveness.

From time to time, it becomes necessary for managers at the first level of supervision to rescue top management from the brink of efficiency. This can best be accomplished by the application of Consequential Retaliation. This obstructive technique is a form of one-upmanship used by various first-level department managers in dealing with each other.

In today's business journals, there are numerous references to the importance of developing and maintaining good peer relationships. The thought of all low-level managers working harmoniously to-

gether is frightening. Thus, in Obstructive Management, it is necessary to create poor peer relationships
which will in turn involve top management in settling
squabbles.

Consequential Retaliation is designed to establish
untenable working relationships among peer groups.
This technique requires a detailed knowledge of
the total organization structure and the accurate
pecking order of executives. It is commonly practiced in two forms: verbal and written. Both
accomplish the same objectives: involving top management in unimportant details and forcing the
brass to pacify apparent disputes.

Since the written approach to Consequential Retaliation is the most widely used, let's review a classic
case involving Henry Fernberg, Supervisor of the
Finishing and Shipping Department, and Arny Gotsell, a salesman for By-Products, Incorporated.

The situation in this case arose subtly enough
when Arny wrote the following memo to Henry:

```
Subject:  Parts on Loading Dock
Date:     September 10
To:       Henry Fernberg, Supervisor,
          Finishing and Shipping
          Department

  While touring the plant yesterday, I
noticed my order of By-Products, which was
supposedly shipped two days ago, still
sitting on the loading dock.
```

```
We cannot live with that kind of service,
Henry! Please look into it.

                              Arny Gotsell
```

This memo landed on Henry's crowded desk just after he had seen an announcement in the plant's paper that Vern Volume, Vice-President of Manufacturing, was about to attend a planning and decision-making course to learn how to improve work output. This indicator of impending efficiency was enough to force Henry into initiating Consequential Retaliation. Pushing the rest of his work aside, Henry quickly dashed off the following memo to Arny Gotsell:

```
Subject:  Your Memo of the 10th
Date:     September 12
To:       Arny Gotsell, Salesman

    The order you referred to as "sitting on
the loading dock" is there because we can-
not read the shipping address on the form
you sent in.
    We can't be expected to ship with im-
proper instructions from salesmen!
                           Henry Fernberg

cc:  Ralph Goodfellow, Field Sales Manager
```

The astute student of obstructive management should note Henry's subtle carboning to the sales-

185

man's manager. This is the opening gambit in the application of Consequential Retaliation. This seemingly innocent act caused Ralph Goodfellow to blast into Arny Gotsell's office two days later, waving the carbon copy and shouting, "What the hell is going on? Didn't you print the shipping address?" to which Arny replied, "In bold face caps. Those jerks just can't read. But don't worry, I'll take care of it."

Arny then cancelled the next three sales calls he was to make and proceeded to carefully word the following memo:

```
Subject:  Reading Efficiency
Date:     September 14
To:       Henry Fernberg, Supervisor,
          Finishing and Shipping Depart-
          ment

   The label you referred to in your memo
of the 12th was carefully printed in capital
letters! I suggest that you teach your per-
sonnel how to read so our customers can get
their orders on time.

                         Arny Gotsell

cc:  Sam Shippit, Plant Superintendent
     Ralph Goodfellow, Field Sales Manager
```

Arny's memo was received two days later. Almost simultaneously, Henry's boss Sam Shippit arrived at Henry's office demanding that he let Arny know that the shipping clerks were all good readers and that they had all passed their high-school equivalency examination! This outburst by his boss caused Henry to realize that his obstructive technique was beginning to pay dividends. He was confident now that Consequential Retaliation was working. He quickly responded to Arny's latest memo in the following manner:

```
Subject:   Reading Comprehension Program
Date:      September 16
To:        Arny Gotsell, Salesman

    This is to inform you that all shipping
clerks completed a certified course in
reading comprehension last month. Further-
more, they have all passed with distinction
the high-school equivalency examination.
Despite their proficiency, it is not pos-
sible to understand your instructions. I
suggest that you take a course in penman-
ship.

                         Henry Fernberg

cc:  Sam Shippit, Plant Superintendent
     Ralph Goodfellow, Field Sales Manager
     Donald Duckit, Regional Sales Manager
```

Regional Manager Donald Duckit reacted almost instantaneously to the carbon copy of this latest memo. He was not going to stand for some shipping clerk criticizing one of his star salesmen. He immediately called Ralph Goodfellow and instructed him to take whatever action he deemed appropriate to preserve Arny's fine reputation. Ralph, needless to say, was quick to jump to Arny's defense. He personally dashed off the following memo to Henry Fernberg:

```
Subject:  Defamation of Character
Date:     September 18
To:       Henry Fernberg, Supervisor,
          Finishing and Shipping Depart-
          ment

   By questioning the validity of Arny Got-
sell's assurance that he had properly com-
plied with the required procedure in the
completion of shipping instructions, you
are endangering his reputation. I wish to
assure you that the Sales Department will
go to any lengths to support one of its star
salesmen. Unfounded allegations are merely
an indication of your inability to perform.

                        Ralph Goodfellow

cc:  Donald Duckit, Regional Sales Manager
     Sam Shippit, Plant Superintendent
     Paul Packit, Plant Manager
```

Here the student of Obstructive Management should note that the memo exchange has moved up one level in the hierarchy. No longer is Arny Gotsell even involved or carboned; also, the original subject has been totally lost somewhere in the exchange.

When Paul Packit received his copy of this most recent memo, he hit the ceiling. His own words are unprintable, but in essence they intimated that salesmen are prima donnas, sales managers are numskulls, and the plant would be better off without the entire sales force. He ordered Sam Shippit to make the plant's position clear to the sales force.

Sam, who himself had little use for sales types, quickly complied by firing off the following memo:

```
Subject:   Erroneous Allegations
Date:      September 20
To:        Ralph Goodfellow, Field Sales
           Manager
```

Your attack on the plant's ability to perform was totally unwarranted. Keep in mind that if we did not produce all these by-products, you would have nothing to sell!

Our production is at peak efficiency and the quality is at an all-time high. If sales would spend less time entertaining and concentrate on selling By-Products, we might be able to unclog our warehouse.

Sam Shippit

```
cc:  Paul Packit, Plant Manager
     Donald Duckit, Regional Sales Manager
     Roger Rightman, Vice-President of
     Marketing
```

Note should be taken here that Henry Fernberg was not mentioned in this most recent memo, and he has lost his position even on the carbons. Consequential Retaliation has now moved even further up the hierarchy to the vice-presidential level.

When Roger Rightman received his copy of this memo, he recognized that he had a real crisis on his hands. He had recently attended a seminar on the "Evolution of the Marketing Concept" and decided that the problem was purely one of the plant's lack of understanding of the value of the marketing concept and the role of the sales organization in servicing customer needs.

Based on this assumption and with the concurrence of the President, Roger quickly structured a one-week course entitled "The Integration of Manufacturing and Sales within the Marketing Concept." He ordered all members of the sales organization to stop writing to the plant until the outcome of this conference was settled. A date was quickly set and the list of mandatory attendees by order of the President included Vern Volume, Vice-President of Manufacturing; Paul Packit, Plant Manager; Sam Shippit, Plant Superintendent; Donald Duckit, Regional Sales Manager; and Ralph Goodfellow, Field Sales Manager. Naturally Roger Rightman would lead the conference. Totally uninvolved in these proceedings were the two originators of Consequential Retaliation: Henry Fernberg and Arny Gotsell.

The date for the conference conflicted with Vern Volume's attendance at the Planning and Decision-making Course. Thus, Henry Fernberg had fully accomplished his original obstructive objective. It also tied up the time of all the major managers in the company, which caused further complications in sales and production.

The lesson to be learned from this application of Consequential Retaliation is that, by involving successively higher levels of management, a minor problem can be escalated beyond belief. Each attempt at retaliation further clouds or obscures the original issue until finally it is totally forgotten. Through Consequential Retaliation, the practitioner attempts to force action at a low level by informing the next higher level of the discrepancy. The implication is that the low-level manager will respond more rapidly due to fear of his own supervisor than through a desire to correct an error.

In the case just described, it was later learned that a mail clerk had accidentally spilled a cup of coffee on the original order form, erasing most of the instructions. Had it not been for Henry Fernberg's diligent application of Obstructive Management, this whole incident and the resulting inefficiency could never have taken place.

# 21: DILIGENT INDECISIVENESS

THE BIG BOY BOILER
Company operated a huge plant located on the riverbank just north of New Orleans. Its prime product was big boilers used in ships and large buildings. The plant had been in existence since the early 1920's and provided employment for some three hundred workers from two nearby communities.

Because of the nature of its product, the plant was constructed with vast areas of open floor space for construction and movement of the heavy boilers. Large, long, low buildings were sprawled along the riverbank with doors leading to docks where barges could be loaded with products.

The plant operated on a two-shift basis—seven A.M. to three P.M. and three P.M. to eleven P.M. During the remainder of the night, nobody was on duty except the watchman at the main gate—because no

# CONTROLLING

one would want to disrupt the operation of the plant that financially supports a major segment of the population of two small towns.

One morning as the first shift was filing into work, a worker made a startling discovery. As he entered the main assembly room, he almost fell headlong into an immense hole that had appeared overnight in the center of the floor. He raced back out of the room to tell the other workers to come and look at the hole.

When the foreman arrived, he found all the workers standing around the edge of the huge hole looking bewildered. "What are we supposed to do?" they chimed almost in unison.

"Beats the hell out of me," replied the foreman. "This is the damnedest thing I've ever seen. I'll call the Shift Superintendent."

So the Shift Superintendent was called. He came racing into the main room to find the workers and the foreman all standing around the edge of the huge hole. "What are we going to do?" they shouted.

The Shift Superintendent scratched his head and said, "That's the biggest damned hole I've ever seen. I'd better call the Plant Manager."

So he called the Plant Manager, who rushed to the main room to find the workers, the foreman, and the Shift Superintendent all standing around the edge of the massive hole and gazing into its depths. "What are we going to do?" they clamored. The Plant Manager wrung his hands and beads of perspiration broke out on his forehead. "That hole is

194

much too large for me to cope with. I'm sure the Vice-President of Manufacturing better be told about this."

So the Vice-President of Manufacturing was called. Fortunately, he was in a nearby town playing golf, so he drove right over. When he arrived, he found the workers, the foreman, the Shift Superintendent, and the Plant Manager all standing transfixed around this huge hole. "What are we going to do?" they shouted.

Calmly, and with the authority of his office, the Vice-President of Manufacturing responded, "Fill the damn thing in." He was used to making decisions, since he makes all of them at Big Boy Boiler Company.

This brief story illustrates in the most straightforward way possible the results of Diligent Indecisiveness. This Obstructive Management Technique can completely stifle an organization's ability to make decisions except at the highest level. All of the workers and lower-level managers were perfectly willing to work, but totally unwilling to make a decision.

Over the years, top obstructive managers have learned that one of the surest ways to halt progress within any organization is to force workers and low-level managers to live in constant fear of making a wrong decision.

Diligent Indecisiveness is the Obstructive Controlling Technique most commonly used to achieve such results. Its main value is that it can be applied at almost any level of management and creates a working environment in which subordinate managers are diligent in the pursuit of routine tasks, yet totally indecisive when faced with any exception. Also, as students of Obstructive Management can readily grasp, this concept goes far toward preserving managerial jobs since, if no work can progress without a decision, the manager becomes a critical element in the entire work process.

Initiation of Diligent Indecisiveness requires proper conditioning. It is not something which can suddenly be decided upon with any high degree of expected results. This is to say, a manager who is delegating decision authority and responsibility downward cannot then suddenly revert to an autocratic approach to decision making.

To develop a climate in which Diligent Indecisiveness can thrive, a good starting point is the preparation of job descriptions. When structuring job descriptions for subordinates or workers, it is important to spell out plainly the various areas of responsibility. But be extremely vague concerning the delegation of the necessary authority to carry out the function. For example, a maintenance engineer might be given, via his job description, the responsibility of keeping equipment in good operating condition at all times. However, the same job description would be extremely vague concerning his real authority to purchase the necessary parts. This conflict between responsibility and authority to act causes the low-level manager or worker to be extremely cautious in making decisions.

196

Once the job description has been established, the next conditioning step for the obstructive manager is to wait for a subordinate to originate any action which would indicate he may have made a decision on his own. The minute the subordinate makes anything but the most minute decision, the obstructive manager must remind him firmly that decisions of this magnitude have to be made at a higher level. It seldom takes more than one or two such reminders until a subordinate learns that before he makes a move, he'd better check it out with his boss. If this thought is constantly drilled into subordinates, the fear of being wrong and suffering the consequences will far overshadow the workers' desire to accomplish any objective whatsoever.

The benefits of this approach to the obstructive manager are that he is constantly kept busy making decisions and subordinates will always remain subordinates, since the only way for a subordinate to grow on a job is to be able to make decisions—be they right or wrong—and learn from experience.

Diligent Indecisiveness has been employed successfully in all fields of endeavor. Evidence of its application can readily be seen in salesmen's inability to plan their own time and make decisions concerning pricing negotiations. Even in such areas as the university campus, professors cannot decide on the content of their courses, but are governed by arbitrary decisions made at far higher echelons.

Thus, the student of Obstructive Management should take particular note of this technique and its great value in firmly establishing managerial authority. Whenever a worker or a subordinate manager says something to the effect that "I'd better check that out with the boss," you can be fairly certain that Diligent Indecisiveness is being effectively employed in one form or another to assure higher-level management of continued employment.

# 22: EXUBERANT DEMORALIZATION

THERE COMES A TIME in the career of every obstructive manager when, through no fault of his own, he is faced with the problem of controlling the performance of a truly brilliant subordinate.

This usually happens when the obstructionist transfers to become head of a department where a star performer is lurking in the background, or when the personnel department accidentally hires a high potential person from the outside and assigns him or her to the obstructionist.

In either case, it is an extremely traumatic experience for the obstructionist. High potential or star performers are always a threat to Obstructive Management. Their creative and innovative abilities tend to overshadow lackluster department efforts. Occasionally, they are recognized by top management and rapidly promoted to positions where their zeal reflects on the total organization's effectiveness, much to the detriment of the status quo. An obstructionist cannot ignore the high potentials, since star performers have a nasty way of being noted even in confused organizations. By the same token, he cannot discourage or downgrade the star because to do so would jeopardize his own position. Hence, he must nullify the brilliant producer in such a way that no blame can be placed on himself.

Until recent years, controlling and eventually eliminating brilliant subordinates has been a major problem for obstructionists. Some attempts were made to reduce their effectiveness by assigning them increasingly more difficult and complex tasks. However, the high potentials viewed this as a challenge and a further opportunity to demonstrate their abilities.

Other obstructive managers tried to ignore their stars and concentrate their efforts on attempting to promote their more mediocre workers. This approach never met with much success, due to the old adage concerning hiding one's light under a basket. Managers who had attempted it were often accused of hiding their star performers so that the top talent would remain to enhance the output of the obstructive manager's department.

Fortunately, today's obstructionist no longer has to be concerned with disposing of super-producers. The serious work done by behavioral scientists in the area of motivation theory—when properly misapplied—can quickly remedy the threat of brilliance.

Two of the most effective behavior-shaping techniques are Positive Reinforcement and Feedback. These, when coupled with psychologists' observations concerning man's need for peer acceptance and approval, make up the Obstructive Controlling Technique of Exuberant Demoralization.

To understand and appreciate the significance of this advance properly, let's examine the implications of positive reinforcement, feedback, and peer acceptance in layman's terms.

*Positive reinforcement,* the behavioral scientists tell us, is a technique used to reinforce or reward good behavior. The more often a good behavior is rewarded, the more often it will be repeated. *Feedback* is simply the manager supplying some signal or means by which an individual can recognize that he or she has accomplished something. *Peer acceptance and approval* means that workers want to be liked or at least approved of by co-workers. They want to belong to a group and do not wish to be left out on their own.

By teaching these three valid motivational concepts, the behavior scientists have, perhaps unwittingly, provided obstructive managers with a powerful method for eliminating stellar performers.

Exuberant Demoralization is the misapplication of all three of these principles, resulting in demotivation. In the lexicon of the obstructionist, positive reinforcement means over-rewarding and over-praising one employee for good behavior at the expense of all other group members. Feedback becomes the manager supplying excessive signals heralding the most minor accomplishments. Peer acceptance and approval translates into peer suppression in which all group members are constantly forced to look up to the examples being set by the star performer, thus ostracizing him from the rest of the group. These three concepts, working in consort, produce Exuberant Demoralization. This, in turn, unleashes a demotivating force powerful enough to suppress even the most dazzling performer.

The first obstructionist to use this three-pronged approach to demotivate was Clarence Pondor, sometimes referred to as the Father of Exuberant Demoralization.

Clarence had always been a practicing obstructionist and in his early years gained an enviable reputation as a deep thinker and student of human relations. Actually, Clarence's real motivation for making an in-depth study of human relations was to seek a solution to the age-old problem posed by the star performer. Clarence himself had suffered through an agonizing experience when his attempts to suppress a high potential subordinate had almost cost him his job.

One day, quite by accident, a *Harvard Business Review* article describing the feedback theory, a University of Michigan personnel quarterly discussing the reinforcement theory, and a dissertation from a psychologist concerning peer-group pressures all arrived on Clarence's desk at the same time. As with all great moments of invention, the concept of mis-application of these three approaches came to Clarence in a flash of brilliance. Thus, Exuberant Demoralization was born.

Clarence, anxious to test the validity of his new concept, took a risk uncommon among obstructive managers and actually volunteered to accept a high-potential candidate that the Personnel Department had accidentally hired.

Shrewdly, Clarence put him to work with a group of people approximately his own age who were engaged in developing business systems for the corporation. Up to this point, the output of this group had been comfortingly less than spectacular.

Within the first two weeks, the dazzling performance turned in by the high potential employee began to have its effect. The systems he designed were truly creative and produced almost immediate savings to the company. Clarence realized it was time to test Exuberant Demoralization.

He immediately instituted a weekly Monday morning meeting of the systems group at which attendance was mandatory. These meetings, combined with interoffice memos and informal get-togethers, served as a launching device for over-positive reinforcement and excessive feedback concerning the activities of his new star performer.

At each meeting, Clarence would heap praise on

his high potential, often suggesting that others in the group adopt his work habits, use his self-planning methods, and even copy his mode of dress. Frequently Clarence would call on his shining light to brief his peers concerning some innovative but demanding approach he had taken in systems analysis.

During the week, Clarence continued his barrage of feedback and reinforcement by means of memos to his hotshot, with carbons going to the rest of the group. Each memo surpassed the previous one in its reinforcement of superior behavior and documentation of results achieved. At every opportunity —in the corridor, at the water cooler, or in the men's room—Clarence would tout the performance of the star.

Within the remarkably short span of four weeks, Exuberant Demoralization paid off. The shining light suddenly and almost inexplicably started making grave errors in systems design. At the Monday morning meetings he became reticent, uncommunicative, and shy. Even his appearance waned to a state of dishevelment. He was merely part of the group.

As accurately predicted by Clarence, peer-group pressure had taken its toll. The group, being unable and unwilling to raise itself to the star's level of performance, had forced him to regress to their norm or be ostracized. Clarence's exuberant praise of his high potential employee had demoralized the rest of the group to the point where they had literally served notice on the brilliant performer to either join them or risk bodily attack. Clarence's innovative theory of Exuberant Demoralization had succeeded!

Now obstructive managers need no longer fear a shining light in their midst. Proper and prompt application of Exuberant Demoralization will quickly serve to level outstanding performance and maintain mediocre group norms.

# 23: POLISHED POMPOUSNESS

THE GREATEST COM-
pliment that can be paid to any obstructive manager
is recognition of his control by means of Polished
Pompousness. To say this of a manager means he
has reached the pinnacle of obstructive success.
Through diligent obstructionism he now, in the twi-
light of his career, is able to enjoy his success and
control his organization via the most insidious of all
the Obstructive Techniques.

While this may be the goal of most obstructionists,
very few actually attain it. Only obstructionists who
have ascended to the presidency of their organization or at least the executive vice-presidential level
can effectively employ this controlling technique.

To learn why Polished Pompousness is such a
difficult yet thoroughly rewarding technique, one

must first consider the required atmosphere or climate. First, the obstructionist must be in total control of the organization. This does not mean that he has to be involved with any of the work elements; in fact, it is often advantageous if he knows very little about how the work is actually accomplished.

Second, the top obstructionist must have working with him a carefully selected group of Vice-Presidents who all want to win his favor and eventually his job. These same Vice-Presidents must have been conditioned never to ask questions and always respond immediately to any implied command.

Third, the chief obstructionist must present the proper appearance both personally and in the manner in which his office is appointed. This requirement can generally be met quite easily by employing the proper tailors, manicurists, barbers, and interior decorators.

Fourth, the would-be practitioner must have acquired the proper verbal and nonverbal mannerisms. He should be able to express varying degrees of emotions with the raise of an eyebrow or the tapping of his glasses. His speech should be low-pitched, slow, and contain deliberately long pauses for proper impact.

Fifth and finally, the obstructionist must have two secretaries to care for his every need. One should have been with him for at least twenty-five years, type upwards of one hundred words per minute with no errors, wear long, shapeless dresses, horned-rimmed glasses, and have the attitude that she actually runs the organization. The other secretary should be about twenty-five years old, wear extremely short skirts and see-through blouses, type very rarely, and be very good at serving coffee and mixing drinks.

Given this proper atmosphere or climate, the senior obstructive executive can relax and control via the prestigious principle of Polished Pompousness.

The principle itself is relatively easy to understand. It is generally defined as the involvement of subordinates in quantities of fruitless reports and studies in an effort to be responsive to meaningless or implied demands. In practice, Polished Pompousness requires an adeptness at implementation which is more difficult to acquire. For example, a chief executive could not merely *order* a subordinate to develop a report on an unimportant subject. This would be lacking totally in finesse and would not qualify as Polished Pompousness.

Applied properly, the subordinate must *assume* that the chief executive wants certain actions taken by what he thinks he has heard or by what was never said at all. This suggests obstructive controlling by innuendoes or artfully contrived jargon, which is the true technique of Polished Pompousness.

Fortunately for the advanced student who wishes to learn more about Polished Pompousness, J. Portly Bankton III, President and Chief Executive Officer of Clean Pipes Limited, has just published a brief article in the *Journal of Obstructionism*. Here is a direct quote from his article:

209

First of all, I felt it necessary to establish the proper climate. To do so, I had Bertha, my secretary of long-standing, call in Prince Gregor to redecorate my office.

The Prince was fantastic! He suggested that one whole wall be made to look like a library with fake bookcovers depicting all of the classics. On another wall, he installed a rotating unit which opens to become a complete bar from which Mazy, my newer secretary, can serve drinks—when closed, it becomes teak panelling.

The carpet is three inches deep, wall-to-wall, in royal blue. My old desk has been replaced with a highly polished teakwood table that, of course, never has a piece of paper on it. Comfortable leather chairs, two couches (one of which makes up into a bed), and several marble coffee tables complete the ensemble.

My office has two entrances, one of which is guarded by Bertha and is used by company employees who wish to see me. Mazy supervises the other entrance which leads to a private elevator. Naturally I have a private bathroom complete with tub and shower in case I have to work late.

My immediate staff consists of four Vice-Presidents who all have been with the company for a number of years and who all want my job when I retire. Because of this, they are easily controlled and are constantly seeking some in-

210

dication of my approval. I have found Polished Pompousness to be a most rewarding controlling technique. It creates an aura of excitement for me to see my subordinates hard at work on inappropriate projects.

The first time I applied this advanced Obstructive Technique was about a year ago. My tailor, Ramon of Paris, had just delivered my new $400 dark blue pin-striped suit. Mazy was serving drinks and I was in a very relaxed mood. Looking at myself in the mirror, I realized the image I presented—immaculately groomed gray hair, half-frame glasses, manicured nails, and my new suit, fitted well into the requirements to attempt Polished Pompousness.

After the tailor had left and Mazy had folded up the bar and swished out the door, I rang for Bertha and asked her to call up Lance Climber, my Marketing Vice-President, and see if he could stop by.

This simple request was transmitted by Bertha, as I knew it would be, by her calling Lance and saying, "The President wants to see you immediately."

Lance arrived slightly out of breath, having run up the last flight of stairs rather than waiting for the elevator. I asked him to sit down on the couch across the room while I remained in my chair behind my teak table.

For a full minute, I said nothing. I just gazed

off into space and slowly tapped my glasses on the polished table surface. This was intended to give Lance the opportunity to catch his breath and to appreciate the atmosphere of my office.

Then, very slowly and with a low-pitched, resonant voice, I said, "Lance, it seems to me that we should have a better handle on Corporate Imperativeness. Don't you agree?" Naturally he agreed wholeheartedly without even asking for any further definition of what I was talking about.

Next I asked how he felt we had best proceed in the development of the concept of Corporate Imperativeness. He responded by jumping up and offering to have a study on my desk within one week. Polished Pompousness was working!

One week and God knows how many man-hours of work later, Lance appeared flanked by the Director of Research, the Director of Strategic Planning, and two M.B.A.'s carrying charts labeled Corporate Imperativeness. They proceeded to put on a massive presentation including feedback loops for data communications, trigger points for action plans, and a market study of growth opportunities.

Through it all, I sat confidently behind my teak table, occasionally nodding, raising an eyebrow, or tapping my glasses on the polished surface. When they had finished, I leaned back and contemplated the light fixture in the ceiling

212

for a full minute, giving them time to catch their breath. Then I said, "It seems to me that the real indicators of Corporate Imperativeness lie somewhere in the concept of Linear Extrapolation. Don't you agree?" Naturally, they all agreed heartily, even with such comments as, "Of course, we should have thought of that," and "That's quite obvious to us now." Lance and his team promised to be back with a new presentation in two weeks and practically knocked each other over in an effort to get out the door.

For the past year now, Lance and his everenlarging team have been attempting to guess what I mean by Corporate Imperativeness. Each time I give them a slightly different suggestion which is promptly misunderstood since no one dares to ask what I really hope to accomplish. If they ever did ask, I don't think I could answer. Polished Pompousness is indeed a most rewarding method of controlling for those of us who are fortunate enough to be able to apply it.

# IV

EVALUATING

# 24: PROBABILISTIC IMPLOSION

A REQUISITE OF MODern management practice is the systematic review or evaluation of progress toward established goals. This same principle applies equally to Obstructive Management. Without evaluation, review, and goal setting, the obstructionist has no valid means of charting his progress.

Basically, the obstructionist becomes involved in three types of evaluations. First, he needs to assess the impact his obstructive practices have had on the organization. Second, he must effectively mis-conduct the evaluation of work accomplished by his subordinates; and third, he should periodically conduct a self-evaluation and goal-setting review to chart his own progress and establish new obstructive goals.

Each of these evaluations requires the mastering of

217

a separate set of skills. The true obstructionist will work hard to develop his evaluative skills, using his own ingenuity wherever possible in developing content and format.

The basis for all evaluation is the accurate identification of results which can be measured in some way. The more an obstructionist can do to provide quantifiable data, the easier it will be to determine results.

First, let's consider how the activities of an obstructive manager *can* be measured in terms of impact on the organization. This problem has been discussed in symposiums throughout the world with little real progress being made toward a common solution. In fact, it is highly unlikely that a common solution will ever be found that can serve as a measurement for all obstructionists.

This sense of frustration was felt recently by J. Thurmond Ridgeback, Executive Vice-President of Sickly Products. Another highly unsuccessful year was drawing to a close. Numerous new management positions had been added, while employee turnover zoomed to an all-time high. Profits had diminished, providing an opportunity to eliminate low-level workers. Product quality had slipped, creating jobs for management inspectors, and excess inventory clogged the warehouses due to low morale in the sales organization. All in all, it had been a most spectacular year of Obstructive Management.

Now bonus time was fast approaching and J. Thurmond Ridgeback had no valid means of measuring his obstructive managers in terms of what each had contributed to the implosion of Sickly Products.

Needless to say, each manager felt that he was the major obstructionist. The General Sales Manager argued vehemently that his use of Dynamic Lethargy in controlling his sales force had accounted for the decline in sales and the clogged warehouse. But J. Thurmond Ridgeback could not be sure and therefore could not properly reward the General Sales Manager. Other events beyond the General Sales Manager's control could have contributed to the sales downturn. All year long, obstructive journalists had been predicting doom. Foreign obstructionists entered the market with new technology. Even within Sickly Products, obstructionists in production, engineering, and market research may have helped cause the sales downturn. What was needed was a systems approach to properly allocate responsibility for implosion.

One day by accident J. Thurmond Ridgeback found a brochure on his otherwise spotless desk describing an approach taken by a consulting firm in identifying probabilities of success. In a flash of genius, it came to him that if success could be measured through this process, so could failure. He lost no time in calling the firm of Potley, Potley, and Blum and setting up an appointment.

Potley, Potley, and Blum were scheduled to arrive at Sickly Products the following day, except that Blum did not come. It seemed he is really only a name to make the firm sound larger. Potley and Potley did, however, show up armed with reams of computer print-outs demonstrating quantitative methods of assigning probabilities.

After hearing J. Thurmond Ridgeback's problem, Potley and Potley immediately recommended the standard consulting approach consisting of a six-month need analysis survey for $60,000, followed by a four-month data analysis project for $40,000, which leads to an implementation schedule for another $20,000. All of this caused J. Thurmond Ridgeback to slump dejectedly behind his desk and throw up his hands in a gesture of futility. All he really wanted was a simple method of determining how effective each of his managers had been in obstructing the progress of Sickly Products.

Potley and Potley excused themselves for a brief men's room caucus. Upon returning, they had apparently decided that Sickly Products was not quite ready for a major study and that they would attempt to sell a minor job to gain a foothold for future business. Their new proposal was simple and direct. Borrowing a process from a well-known market-forecasting technique, they presented the concept of Probabilistic Implosion as a solution to J. Thurmond Ridgeback's needs.

To apply it, they suggested that each manager reporting to J. Thurmond Ridgeback write out a list of results that he felt could happen if he properly applied Obstructive Techniques. A list might include such results as a decrease in product quality, drop in

220

corporate profits, or an increase in personnel turnover, etc.

Potley and Potley then recommended that once
each list was complete, the individual obstructionist
catalog the actions he had taken over the year that
might in some way have contributed to the negative
result. Each manager was instructed to think only
in terms of specific programs or systems he had personally introduced. Potley and Potley were very firm
about only counting major efforts, such as the introduction of Flexible Rigidity as an organizing system
or Controlling via Dynamic Lethargy.

The next and final step recommended was for
each manager to take a flying guess at rating the
probability of impact caused by each program or
action taken. Potley and Potley illustrated this by an
example: If one manager had introduced Prolific
Ponderousness within his department, the total impact upon the whole organization might be assessed
at a twenty percent probability of impact. If this
same manager had also applied Flexible Rigidity,
he could possibly claim another ten percent probability of impact. Controlling via Dynamic Lethargy
could earn him fifteen percent more probability of
impact for a total annual probability of forty-five
percent.

Potley and Potley were quick to point out that it
rarely is possible for one individual to earn a rating
as high as forty-five percent. Exceptionally high rat-
ings are generally registered only by Presidents of
small companies or extremely obstructive Executive

Vice-Presidents. This made J. Thurmond Ridgeback feel very good, anticipating the high rating he could develop for himself.

The consultants recommended that before assigning percentages to the potential impact obstructive actions may have had on the organization, each manager must consider his position in the hierarchy, the number of people managed, the relative importance of the functions being performed, the actions taken by other obstructionists, and the positive counter-measures employed by efficient managers.

At this point, J. Thurmond Ridgeback became rightfully concerned. Knowing his managers as well as he did, he realized that they were never going to honestly evaluate their own impact. Each would claim an unrealistically high percentage.

For a short time, it looked as if Potley and Potley would lose the deal. Then the younger Potley came up with the brilliant suggestion of conducting a joint Probability Assessment Seminar. During this seminar, to be conducted by the impartial consultants, each manager would complete a Probabilistic Implosion Evaluation Form (see Figure 6, opposite). These completed forms would be exchanged, and as the result of the ensuing arguments, discussions, and accusations, the participants would arrive at a reasonable estimate of impact.

J. Thurmond Ridgeback was delighted. At last, he had a semi-valid means of measuring obstructive performance. He immediately hired Potley and Pot-

Figure 6:
PROBABILISTIC IMPLOSION EVALUATION

Name _____

Title _____

| Results Affected | Obstructive Actions Taken | % Probability of Impact |
|---|---|---|
| Increased turnover | Prolific Ponderousness | 20% |
| Decreased profit | Flexible Rigidity | 10% |
| Product quality reduction | Diligent Indecisiveness | 5% |
| Excess inventory | Affirmative Abandonment | 4 % |
| | | Total 39 % |

ley to conduct the Probabilistic Implosion Assessment Seminar.

The results of the seminar were highly rewarding despite having to pay Potley and Potley $20,000. With their help, J. Thurmond Ridgeback was able to hold the Percent Probability of Impact for his direct reports down to a minimum of forty percent. This meant that J. Thurmond Ridgeback could personally claim a sixty percent probability of impact for himself and keep most of the bonus money.

# 25: EFFECTIVE DEVALUATION

BEHAVIORAL SCIENTISTS tell us that employees work harder and more efficiently if they are provided with feedback on their performance and are counseled on ways to improve. Because of this, the conduct of annual performance evaluations for subordinates has become an important function of management.

For the obstructive manager, the annual performance review presents yet another opportunity for him to lower subordinates' morale and decrease efficiency. This does not mean that he can merely ignore performance reviews or conduct them in an abusive, negative manner. To accomplish the desired results, he must use both finesse and precision timing.

After years of experimentation with differing formats, content, and timing, it is now generally agreed that the most efficient obstructive approach to conducting performance reviews is Effective Devaluation. This technique capitalizes on the natural reluctance of managers to level with subordinates concerning their shortcomings. Also, because of the content and timing employed in execution, the strategy effectively devaluates the subordinate's own self-image. This is an important point since the loss of self-image is a thing which impacts upon the subordinate himself—something for which the manager cannot be held accountable.

The leading proponent of Effective Devaluation is Ms. Clara Coacham, who for the past few years has been conducting a series of public seminars teaching managers to employ this obstructive devaluating technique properly. The brochure describing the course states plainly that participants who complete the program will be able to:

1. Plan and organize a devaluating review
2. Phrase obstructive statements
3. Successfully avoid developmental issues
4. Establish the climate for destruction of subordinates' self-image
5. Satisfy company requirements for mandatory reviews

The brochure also gives a glowing profile of Ms. Coacham, listing her degrees in obstructive personnel management and expounding on her years of experience with a number of blue-chip corporations.

On the back of the brochure are the following

short testimonial statements freely given by past participants:

"A truly rewarding experience. Ms. Coacham is the greatest!"—Bud Dudley, General Manager, Dudley Construction Company.

"Never realized devaluation could be so easy. Bless you, Ms. Coacham!"—Dan Rancid, Personnel Manager, Whiffy Cheese Company.

"Clara, Clara, Clara! Wow! What a week!"—Stanley Swinger, Marketing Manager, Peek Pix Incorporated.

Because of these glowing testimonials and a great brochure, it seemed appropriate to take the three-day course and report on its relevance for students of Obstructive Management.

The seminar was held at the Rondezvous Hotel, located just past the intersection of I-20 and I-75 outside Atlanta, Georgia. This location was chosen, it seems, because of its proximity to an airport and Clara's desire to keep the participants to herself and away from the temptations of a downtown hotspot.

Registration was set for 6:00 P.M. on Sunday in time for a welcoming cocktail party. The check-in process followed pretty much the normal routine: paying the fee, collecting pre-meeting materials, and pinning on a misspelled name tag.

Clara was there to greet each registrant with a lingering handshake and a pleasantry such as, "I know you will find this to be a most meaningful experience. So happy to have you with us."

Clara is an apparent blonde of ample proportions.

Speculation on her age ranged from a low of twenty-five, submitted by a snowy-haired General Manager, to a high of forty-five, loudly stated by a mini-skirted participant who had instantly collected a circle of admirers.

The cocktail party served its purpose of getting the group lubricated. As usual, a great deal of time was devoted to credential setting by participants who seemed to feel it important to let everyone know of their expertise in Obstructive Management and that they were attending only as observers.

With cocktails and dinner out of the way, we assembled in the meeting room for an official welcome by Clara. She outlined the program for the next three days, stressing the importance of interaction. Then she distributed a three-page article on "Planning the Devaluation Review" for homework.

Classes started promptly at 8:30 A.M. Monday. All participants were present, though several felt the night had ended far too quickly.

The first period, which lasted up to a much-needed coffee break at 10:00 A.M., was devoted to a brief lecture by Clara on "Why Companies Establish Performance Reviews as a Mandatory Policy." The key points covered were:

1. To create additional jobs for file clerks in the personnel department
2. To gather evidence prior to dismissal of an employee

3. To use as proof when promoting a relative or friend
4. To use as a measurement of morale and dissatisfaction
5. To confirm management's subjective estimates of employees' abilities

Each of these points were explored at great length by participants in discussion groups, the objective being for each team to feedback actual uses of performance reviews within their own companies which tied in with Clara's overall list. As it turned out, Clara was particularly interested in the feedback for its use as documentation in a new book she is preparing.

After the coffee break and up until lunch, attention was focused on planning and organizing the devaluation review. The chief planning considerations were timing, sequencing, selecting location, and obstructive objectives.

Concerning timing, Clara strongly emphasized that the review never should be held prior to or exactly on the anniversary of the employee's date of employment. To do so would be in line with the employee's expectations and thus lose an opportunity for creating dissatisfaction. The recommended timing turned out to be three or four months past the employment anniversary. Time of day was also discussed, with a general agreement being reached that 4:45 P.M. was most appropriate. This places maximum pressure on the employee and also gives the obstructive manager a valid excuse for terminating the interview in time to beat the five o'clock rush hour.

Sequencing involves the scheduling of subordinates in such a way that internal conflicts will develop over who is reviewed first and who follows who in order of preconceived importance.

As for location, there seemed to be several acceptable approaches, ranging from the manager's own office to standing around the water cooler. One significant point that came out of discussions on location sites was that wherever the review was held, there must be opportunities for distractions such as phone calls, messages, or other interruptions.

Clara was quite emphatic that the obstructive objective for holding the review should be planned carefully in advance. Such pre-planning enables the manager to predict the results of the review and often to complete the actual forms weeks ahead of time. As proof of this, Clara described the case of an obstructionist who had successfully pre-written reviews for all of his employees for the next five years. At review time, he merely produced the appropriate pre-prepared form and the whole review was finished in a matter of minutes.

After lunch, the program emphasis shifted to the real heart of the obstructive performance review—the interview itself. The objective of the afternoon session was to prepare the participants for role-playing reviews they would conduct the following morning. Clara had developed a list of obstructive statements to be practiced for the role playing. She also described in great detail the proper attitudinal approach to be taken by the manager in relation to his objective. The recommended attitudes ranged from a jovial kidding approach (for the manager who wishes to stress the unimportance of the whole review) to the somber pedantic approach (communicating impending doom).

The homework assignment for Monday night was to take Clara's list of obstructive statements and write out the probable thoughts of each subordinate as he hears them. Here is the complete list with appropriate interpretations:

1. MANAGER: "Ha, ha, he, he, he, ho, ho— it's that time of year again!"

   EMPLOYEE: *He sure takes it lightly, big joke, just a routine.*

2. MANAGER: "Golly, I wish we could have gotten together before this, but I've been so busy with important matters."

   EMPLOYEE: *On an importance scale of one to ten, I must rate zero.*

3. MANAGER: "Let's get this over quickly, I have another appointment in ten minutes."

   EMPLOYEE: *Sounds like a rubber-stamp operation.*

4. MANAGER: "Just initial these forms so

we can meet personnel re-
quirements—you and I both
know the kind of job you
are doing."

EMPLOYEE: *I know, and you apparently
don't even care.*

5. MANAGER: "How is your golf game—
ha, ha, ha, ha—"

EMPLOYEE: *When the hell do I have time
to play golf?*

6. MANAGER
TO
SECRETARY: "Miss Jones, this won't take
long, so see if you can get my
call through to Mr. Bigger."

EMPLOYEE: *Here comes the fast shuffle.*

7. MANAGER: "Let's confine our discussion
to your failure to meet the
goals I set. I don't want to
hear any excuses."

EMPLOYEE: *What's the use of even talking?*

8. MANAGER: "We don't need to spend a
lot of time on this. I have already rated you good or superior on everything. You
know your own weaknesses."

EMPLOYEE: *My biggest weakness is
working here.*

9. MANAGER: "Personnel has sent me all
these forms, so let's see if
we can figure them out."

EMPLOYEE: *He sure has put a lot of
thought into this.*

10. MANAGER: "Ha, ha, ha, it is a good thing my secretary reminded me that it is review time again or I never would have gotten around to it. My how time flies!"

EMPLOYEE: *If I hadn't reminded his secretary, they both would have forgotten!*

The Tuesday role-playing sessions were a huge success. Participants were paired and assigned roles of the subordinate or the manager. Devaluation reviews were conducted and then criticized by the entire class. A lot of good learning took place and it was amazing to see how skillfully the role-playing managers inserted Clara's list of obstructive statements into the interviews.

The role-playing subordinates were asked to describe their feelings concerning the tactics employed and all but one agreed that their self-image was deflated and morale lowered. The exception was our mini-skirted participant who felt that in the real world, no man could possibly overlook her potential or obstruct her progress. Clara quickly attacked this remark by pointing out that someday the female participant might just have to work for another woman, who most certainly would obstruct her progress.

Wednesday was devoted to a review of the subjects covered, and culminated with Clara summarizing the characteristics of Effective Devaluation: Plan and organize the devaluating review, employ obstructive statements, and avoid developmental counseling. This will diminish the subordinate's self-image while satisfying any mandatory requirements the company may have for an annual performance review.

All in all, it was a most interesting seminar. Ms. Clara Coacham outdid herself in an attempt to communicate fully, even to the extent of lengthy night sessions with selected participants. For students of Obstructive Management, Effective Devaluation is definitely a must in their repertoire of techniques.

# 26: OBJECTIVE INTROSPECTION

THE SERIOUS OBSTRUC-
tive manager must have a means of measuring his
own progress and development. With the rapid rate
of change taking place in all fields of endeavor,
today's obstructionist could find his techniques obsolete within the next five years. There is nothing worse
than an obsolete obstructionist! His efforts could no
longer be a detriment to an organization and he certainly could not qualify for advancement. Thus, this
final chapter is devoted to preventing obsolescence.

Up to the present, development of obstructive talents has been left up to the individual. Some of the
more introverted obstructionists have conducted
lengthy self-analysis sessions to identify their true
aspirations, strengths, weaknesses, and accomplishments. This has not proven satisfactory, however,
since few if any will admit failure, even to them-

selves. What is needed is a rallying point for obstructionists to provide continuous development and add
status to the profession.

Fortunately for the obstructionists of the future,
an organization which will respond to this developmental need is presently being formed. It is called
the Obstructive Management Association, and its
founder is Doctor Paul J. Finkley. Dr. Finkley was
formerly Executive Vice-President of Nowhere In-
dustries, and has devoted most of his working life to
the furtherance of obstructive technology.

The author found Dr. Finkley at a large printing
shop in Hohokus, New Jersey. The shop's name is
Obstructive Press and it forms the cornerstone of the
future Obstructive Management Association. Dr.
Finkley graciously consented to the following interview.

AUTHOR:    The concept of an Obstructive
           Management Association is in-
           deed an exciting one, Dr.
           Finkley, but why start it with
           a print shop?

DR. FINKLEY:  Obstructive Press, or O. Press
           for short, is *the* most important
           function an association can
           have. Printing is a critical part
           of association work. Brochures,
           letters, membership cards,
           awards, and press releases are

what make an association tick.

AUTHOR: What about seminars, research libraries, and competent faculty?

DR. FINKLEY: All in good time. Good promotion is far more important than good content. Just look at this new brochure. It offers a one-week seminar at an exclusive hotel, plus membership in O. M. A. for $600. Also, the option is given of sending a company team for $1,600, which includes a company membership.

AUTHOR: Very impressive—but what subjects are being covered?

DR. FINKLEY: Just listen to this list of down-to-earth content for our seminar on Objective Introspection:

The Obstructive Job Description, at Present and in the Future.

Analysis of Organizational Obstructive Climate.

Introspective Analysis Techniques.

Obstructive Goal Setting and Planning.

AUTHOR: That's a great list of subjects, but where are you going to find the faculty to teach them?

DR. FINKLEY: That's the beauty of an association. Anyone who joins an association already feels he is knowledgeable in the specialized field. He is really just looking for a chance to prove it. Thus, all you have to do to run a seminar is publish a good-looking brochure, find one big-name speaker who will act as a conference leader, and the participants will run their own seminar.

AUTHOR: What about text and hand-out materials?

DR. FINKLEY: Admittedly, the first time a new seminar is run it may be a little light. However, we make a practice of covertly recording each session. These recordings are transcribed and become the content of future seminars.

AUTHOR: Isn't that illegal? What if a participant found out?

DR. FINKLEY: It never has been a problem. You see, once a participant has graduated from a seminar he would never attend the same program again. Even if he did find out, we can handle it quickly by giving him the O. Press Award for Outstanding Contribution to a Working Seminar.

AUTHOR: What plans do you have for the future?

DR. FINKLEY: Once we gather enough material, we plan to introduce self-study courses, movies, books, and international obstructive workshops. We can learn a lot from foreign obstructionists, you know. Also, once we have generated sufficient capital, we plan to make grants to selected universities for the establishment of Schools of Obstructology. This will help us maintain our tax-free, non-profit status.

AUTHOR: My, all this sounds exciting. I can see that in the years ahead the Obstructive Management Association will play a major role in the development of individual obstructionists throughout the world. I'd like to thank you for granting this interview and wish you the best of luck in this important venture.

DR. FINKLEY: Before you go, I'd like to present you with the first O. Press Award for Outstanding Contribution to Working Seminars.

AUTHOR: You mean—

DR. FINKLEY: Yes, we've taped our whole conversation and also stolen a copy of your text as the start of our library.

Well, as you can see, obstructionists of the future will have little difficulty in maintaining their competency. The profession of Obstructive Management cannot help but rise to greater heights, ultimately saving the free enterprise system from over-efficiency.

Roy S. Farris